THE EXTRAORDINARY *Makeover*

HIDDEN EXPRESSIONS OF THE EVERY DAY WOMAN

LORIE P. WOODRUFF

The author of this book shares information regarding becoming the best person you can be. The information provided is based on the personal philosophy and experience of the author and co-authors. The intent is to provide general information that, when applied, will aid readers in attracting various things they desire in life. In the event that you use any of the information in this book, the author assumes no responsibility for your actions.

Printed in the United States of America

First Printing, 2018

Lorie P. Woodruff

12138 Central Avenue

Suite 494

Bowie, MD 20721

Stay connected with Lorie P. Woodruff at
www.LorieWoodruff.com

Table of Contents

ACKNOWLEDGEMENTS

I give every ounce of thanks to God, my creator, who made it possible for me to give birth to my assignment. Through all the tears, you molded a new woman out of me.

This collaboration would not be possible if these extraordinary women didn't say YES! Alicia R. Mathis, Tnitra King, Raw Wisdom, Salvia Giridhar, Nicole Welton, Kita Holmes, Shakeita Price, Jackie M. Brooks, Keyona Squire, Micola K. Glasgow, Maryanna Eva Lanham, Rhamsye A. Brown, Antoinette Scott, Carrie Jackson, Briele Carter, Dr. Rashida Mendes, and G.G Carter. Thank you for answering the call to write your story. Your stories and life lessons will resonate for a lifetime and change the lives of many women across the world.

I dedicate this book to the Queen and King in my life, mom and dad. Without your encouragement, positive words, and influence, this book would have never been birthed. I send another dedication to the Princesses and Prince in our family, my sisters and brother. You helped keep my energy and laugh ability up and I appreciate the "no filter" approach in all our conversations. To my heavenly Grandma Betty, I continuously hear your encouraging voice. To my earthly Grandma Meg, you keep the humor going and you don't even know it.

Thank you to each reader who invested in *The Extraordinary Makeover: Hidden Expressions Of The Every Day Woman.*

This book was designed and birthed with your greatness in mind.

To the countless motivational speakers, seminars, books, and videos I have absorbed over the years, you have helped shape me into an extraordinary Lorie. I send a special thank you to all the key mentors and teachers who influenced my steps in life and saw more in me than I ever could see in myself. Thank you Trevor Otts, who gave me the best business ideas and courage to bring Lorie TV alive; Bob Yates, who spoke life into my world;

Melanie Bonita, whose book *Daily Dose of Determination and consultation*, changed the direction of my life; Barbara Davis for your swift editing skills; Jami Watkins and Stephen Janey for your slick graphic artistry; Jason Fenwick, for your business advice; Justin Owens for being a true example of leadership, problem solver, and friend; Daniel Bethea and David Turner for listening to me get through my wacky life episodes and new ideas.

To my real estate and forex family, I appreciate working alongside you every day. Because of you, you've helped me form Lorie TV to serve your business and life. And lastly to my TV alter ego, Ms. Woodchuck, keep the glasses on straight, keep everyone on their toes, and stay sharp!

PREFACE

What if I told you that, by the end of this book, I could reveal makeover secrets that could make you more confident, happier, and more attractive? What if I told you, the everyday woman, that you have everything possible to become *irresistible* if you wanted to? Would you spend the time to read the book and get the answers?

Sometimes you have to dig deep to find that hidden glow, passion, and strength. Our version of The Extraordinary Makeover has nothing to do with lashes and lipstick. It's about waking up and being alive, being expressive, and most importantly, being you. It's about healing every false thought you've ever had about personal and business relationships.

It's about discovering your natural ability to be authentic, sensual, and downright irresistible in a way that is true to your soul and inspires others to do the same. It means telling the truth and being real throughout the peaks and valleys we call life. It's about accessing your highest self and living consistently with awareness. Tricks and techniques are cheap. Authentic expressions are exquisite and appealing. We're going for the real deal!

You must take it one day at a time, one hour at a time, one minute at a time. Life isn't always easy. As women, we have the power to make our lives as great as we possibly can. We introduce ***The Extraordinary Makeover: Hidden Expressions Of The Every Day Woman*** to be our everything when we feel like we have nothing left but know that we want to win!

When we decided to write this book, we all agreed to unveil the secrets that make us extraordinary women. While it would have been easy to fill this book about high notes and stories about our wins, that is not the story we desired to tell. These stories are about transparency and true life makeovers. We wanted to share our stories, not to cause you to question who you are or where you've been, because each of our journeys are different.

But we do hope that you will see yourself in these pages, and be open to the lessons we've learned, the opportunities that await you, and the strength that undoubtedly exist in you. It's time to unleash and reveal the extraordinary you!

With an open mind, the world will finally discover how innovative, smart, beautiful, exciting, fun, sexy, and irresistible you really are. Are you ready? Let's go!

CHAPTER 1

INTENTIONAL TEACHINGS

by Alicia R. Mathis

As I was trying to find my way through this thing called life, I found myself suddenly with three cute little girls, which changed the course of my life as I knew it. These were my brother's daughters and I was only eighteen years old when it all started. They were a blessing in disguise, because what would my life be without them? Probably boring and uneventful, as they are the forces of energy that direct my attention to do what I need to do and it's never a dull moment.

It was very natural for my mom and me to raise my nieces, because we are a very close-knit family that looks out for one another. Even throughout my childhood I was always hanging-out at a family member's house, so family values were instilled in me early on in life. Because my mom and family always looked out for me, my instincts of wanting to take care of my nieces were natural when my mom said, "let's take the girls permanently." Before I knew it, I was in the role of co-parenting.

With my upbringing, the nurturing side was a no-brainer, making sure the girls had clothes, their hair was done, they had the vital necessities for school, that we could provide the things they needed, that we impressed upon them to get their education, and teaching them how to be careful in the streets. Financially, I tried to give them everything I could provide and afford. You should have seen their Christmases...I went overboard and so did our entire family. In the mist of spoiling them and giving them everything that I could, I was on the path of enabling them. I spoiled them with monetary and material things, and there's nothing wrong with that, but I should have included spoiling them with more life skills. Although I was an enabler, it was intended to ensure the girls didn't feel like they missed out on anything in their childhood. It worked, at least that's what they tell me. (Smiles)

As the girls got older, I had a paradigm-shift, or an “Aha Moment,” if you will. It became clear that I should have been intentionally teaching the girls more life skills and showing them specifically how to do something and what to do with it. You see, at the time, I didn’t realize that I should have been arming them with the skills to be successful in life; Life Skills. The means to survive when faced with challenges, especially as it relates to managing your finances.

I just assumed that they would view me as their role model and follow the things I did; not necessarily verbatim, but with observation and curiosity for the way I managed life. However, we as parents are so busy just doing, we don’t take the time to show how certain life skills are needed to maintain; like managing their money, for example. One lesson out of this is that if we don’t intentionally teach our children life skills, they will learn through the school of hard knocks. Granted, I was young myself and trying to navigate life and finish my own formal education.

In hindsight, if our generation of parents and their generation of parents never knew to specifically teach such life skills as budgeting and credit, then of course it wouldn’t have come easy for us to think about such things. I had to evolve into my own life cycle to figure this out. I believe life is about cycles and we were never intentionally taught about finances.

Our introduction to finances was our parents telling us to turn off the lights, because we are running up the electric bill. All we knew was that there was apparently an electric bill and our parents paid it. You know children think that money grows on trees. LOL!

I think most people are so pro-education, they think formal education or book smarts will make-up for the life skills we lack. For instance, I believe that formal education does not teach you the skills necessary to handle your finances. They teach the math, the formulation and how to count money, but not how to use it responsibly and that's the part that gets everyone into trouble. Because of that, I am now realizing life skills are just as important, if not more important than formal education.

As a parent, I get it. We make certain that our kids do their homework and get good grades (we call that book smarts). We train them starting from Kindergarten to get good grades in school, study hard so they can get into college, and get a good job. We even reward them for how many A's they get on their report cards. I think formal education is the first piece of the puzzle that everyone gets as it is a cycle that most people have embedded in their daily habits by the time they're adults.

I believe I did a good job of encouraging the idea of formal education to the girls and they have street smarts; however, I wish I would have purposefully focused a little more energy in the life skills/life smarts department. According to Chinese proverbs, "Give a man a fish and you feed him for a day. Teach him how to fish and you feed him for a lifetime".

The other piece of the puzzle is street smarts. It's natural for us as parents to caution our children to be careful in the streets and community, i.e. look both ways before you cross the street, watch your back at all times, if you put your drink down and walk away, do not come back and drink it, and have your keys out for the house before you get out of the car. While I was prepared for book smarts & street smarts, I wasn't conscious enough to directly teach the life skills piece of life.

See, there are book smarts in-which everyone focuses on. Then there are street smarts which are also prevalent in life. We also stress street smarts to our children, so they don't get into trouble. The one component between book smarts and street smarts are life smarts, the one concept no one truly outlines or really takes the time to teach. This becomes the cycle we so desperately need to change.

For example, Millennials and Generation Z (or Zers) have been proven to be unfamiliar with a broad range of life skills.

They are less likely to know how to manage money, open a bank account, save money, how to dress for a job interview, how to cook, sew, make basic home repairs, or communicate effectively. Most do-not process respect, manners or even the proper etiquette to carry out the life skills they are taught. They lack the necessary skills for decision-making, goal-setting, public speaking, preparation for college and career, how to pay for college, resume writing, conflict resolution, business building, problem-solving, confidence-building, time management, and interviewing for jobs. By not intentionally teaching these basic life skills, they become more dependent on us as parents. Especially when it comes to managing money. Not knowing how to manage money can quickly become unmanageable; bad credit, mountains of debt, and no idea how to get out of it. More life skills classes are needed to better prepare them for the future to include business building classes. We as parents should start running game plays about the subject of budgeting alone. Give them scenarios: "You have $2,000 for the month and you have the following items: Mortgage/Rent, car note, insurance, cell phone bill, electric bill, cable, transportation to and from work, buy food and purchase the latest purse or shoes.

Please prioritize and differentiate between your wants and your needs. Oh, not enough money, then part-time job or side hustle it is and no cable, new purse or shoes, because those are wants, not needs. Also remove the bells and whistles from your cell phone plan. Oh, and keep those lights off so you won't run up your electric bill. (You get the idea.)

Fast forward to today, my girls are the reason I became a Financial and Life Coach. Life Coaching is becoming more prevalent in our society as we are seeing more and more coaches appear. I'm a firm believer that we need to intentionally teach life skills with an emphasis on how to manage money and credit to our young kids/young adults. This is an area that is needed amongst Millennials and Generation Z. Proverbs 22:6 - "Train up a child in the way he should go: and when he is old, he will not depart from it."

I believe that out of all the life skills, a focus on finances is the most important, so I made that my subject matter. If a person does not know how to manage their money and if they don't have the right mindset or behavior about money matters, they will not personally achieve economic or personal satisfaction to reach their life goals. They will stay in a continuous pattern of mismanaging money, borrowing money, and diving deeper in debt.

My mindset has totally shifted. Change the way you look at things and the things you look at will change.

I'm of the approach that you don't know what you don't know until someone brings it to our attention, or we grow wiser and start seeking questions, the answers and hopefully the epiphanies start to flow.

In families, we have family gatherings i.e. cookouts, etc., but we don't hold each other accountable enough to the life skills/life smarts that are the key to having a plentiful and abundant life. "Am I my brother's keeper, yes I am". I'm not stating that if you teach people life skills that they won't make any mistakes, on the contrary, but it will certainly make life easier. Life skills assist people to overcome obstacles and help improve their outlook on life. They provide the abilities necessary to set goals, create a plan, build relationships, and personal development.

Life skills are a part of the bigger picture. They can give you that edge when paired with formal education. Life skills helps you play the game and provides more insight into how the game is played in corporate America. They allow us to become more strategic in the work place and in business.

The world needs more experienced and knowledgeable mentors and motivators to guide and provide purpose.

We need more people to show the younger generation that they matter in general.

The road for the girls and I has been filled with love and lessons, and we always have a great time with each other. My nieces became the direct effect of a repetitive cycle. Though the life skills portion has been a bumpy ride and certainly not easy; as the saying goes "Each One Teach One" on the journey to learning and implementing such skills at the adult phase in your life.

As we continue this journey, I pray that the "Aha Moments" keep coming, they have their own paradigm-shifts, and develop a passion for mentoring others. I'll be there to intentionally support them mentally, emotionally, spiritually, and with financial advice to continue to keep them on a path that connects them to a bright future.

Proverbs 4:10-27

10 Hear, my son, and accept my words,

that the years of your life may be many.

11 I have taught you the way of wisdom;

I have led you in the paths of uprightness.

12 When you walk, your step will not be hampered,

and if you run, you will not stumble.

13 Keep hold of instruction; do not let go;

guard her, for she is your life.

14 Do not enter the path of the wicked,

and do not walk in the way of the evil.

15 Avoid it; do not go on it;

turn away from it and pass on.

16 For they cannot sleep unless they have done wrong;

they are robbed of sleep unless they have made someone stumble.

17 For they eat the bread of wickedness

and drink the wine of violence.

18 But the path of the righteous is like the light of dawn,

which shines brighter and brighter until full day.

19 The way of the wicked is like deep darkness;
they do not know over what they stumble.

20 My son, be attentive to my words;
incline your ear to my sayings.
21 Let them not escape from your sight;
keep them within your heart.
22 For they are life to those who find them,
and healing to all their[a] flesh.
23 Keep your heart with all vigilance,
for from it flow the springs of life.
24 Put away from you crooked speech,
and put devious talk far from you.
25 Let your eyes look directly forward,
and your gaze be straight before you.
26 Ponder[b] the path of your feet;
then all your ways will be sure.
27 Do not swerve to the right or to the left;
turn your foot away from evil.

Alicia R. Mathis is a native of Washington, DC and has a passion for helping others, especially young people. Her goal is to help break financial barriers and show young people how to live their best lives. She raised her three nieces and wishes now she had sat them down when they were much younger and taught them the Life Skills she's now teaching others.

Alicia proudly received her Bachelor's degree from Howard University, later her MBA in Financial Management from Southeastern University and is a member of Delta Sigma Theta Sorority, Inc. For ten years, she worked at the Department of Homeland Security managing a $50M budget. She is a top producing real estate professional with fifteen years of experience in the District of Columbia and Maryland.

Her plan is to disrupt the real estate market and continue to assist people with the biggest purchase of their lives. She loves entrepreneurship and her journey in real estate provides an opportunity to be your own boss, create wealth, build a legacy, and have a flexible schedule.

Along with real estate, Alicia reaches out to others as a Life and Financial Coach through leadership and financial teachings. Through these programs she hopes to end the cycle of financial illiteracy that plagues the Millennials and members of Generation Z.

Alicia loves spending time with her husband Marc, mother, nieces, step daughters, brother, great niece and great nephew, and the rest of her close-knit family. She loves to fix and flip homes, travel and looks forward to doing more of it!

Stay connected with me on Facebook @ aliciamathissellshomes

CHAPTER 2

FROM DEVASTATION TO REVELATION

by Tnitra King

The sweat dripped down my face as my heart raced. My heart raced faster than the Reggae music that pounded in the background from my Zumba class. My heart raced, and my body heated up as I tried to process the information that I had just received: my husband was cheating on me.

In June 2009, I had received a call that my boyfriend had been in an accident, but not to fret, as everything was okay.

With that, I took my time getting to the hospital, but as I arrived, I got a really funny feeling that although I had been told everything was going to be okay, something in the air just wasn't right. I walked into the hospital warily and asked for my boyfriend. As I thought, it was a disaster. My boyfriend was bruised, with cracked ribs, and an almost-severed left leg. All the other things were just minor; however, I couldn't even imagine what we were about to go through. While I was more than thankful that he was alive, I was terrified of what was to come. I just couldn't even imagine how this was going to impact his jovial spirit, and our life, but I was up for the challenge because this was the love of my life. I walked into Intensive Care and got ready for the ride of my life.

Three months later, in September 2009, we got ready for our wedding. By then, the good news was, so far, my boyfriend was able to keep his leg. We had gone through almost four surgeries. I was heartbroken as I saw him lying in bed, miserable over what had transpired up until now. I could only imagine what he was going through, how he was feeling. I was distraught but was ready to ride it out because I was his support system as he was mine.

The wedding was beautiful, even though it did hurt my soul that my husband could not walk me down the aisle.

I married him in a wheelchair, against all of the advice from family and friends not to. They didn't want to see me in such a disarray, facing challenge after challenge, taking care of someone for the rest of our lives. I understood where they were coming from, but how could I leave the man I loved just because of some health issues? In my mind, I was in love and I loved hard, and there was nothing that would stop that, even something of this magnitude. Love prevailed, and we were married.

Our first couple of years were challenging, with all of my husband's health issues. There were six additional surgeries, skin grafts, and merging bone together to ensure his leg stayed in place. On top of all that came the medical bills, piling higher than Mt. Everest. However, even with all of the strain and challenge, we had awesome support systems and our love shined for each other. That's what kept us going, LOVE, or so I thought. We decided we wouldn't worry about the bills. Our goal was to work to get him well. Even against what the doctors said, we had faith that *he would walk again*. Each day was a struggle, but I was there as the support system, the wife, the nurse, the lover, the friend.

Fast forward to 2012, and through hard work and faith in God, my husband had regained the use of his left leg.

All of the pain, crying, trauma, worries, devastation—it was all in the past as my husband trained to run a 5K. Doctors had said he would never walk again; in fact, they didn't even think he would keep his leg, but now he was training for a 5K! Completely a miracle. It was beautiful, life was amazing, and I was just thrilled about this amazing journey that we were about to begin. I had even thought, on our 5-year wedding anniversary, maybe we should have a small wedding so that he could walk me down the aisle.

The ability to walk brought him a new sense of self, and a new sense of accomplishment and confidence. Rightfully so! But I also began to notice the longer looks in the mirror, the elongated times alone, the extended time on the cell phone. But I figured, hey, let the man live, especially with all that he's been through. Along with that, his extra weight started falling off, and with it the pressure for me to join the weight loss journey began, which made me unhappy. I thought, I loved ALL of you at your largest, but somehow I'm not good enough because you are losing weight?!

The tears continued to fall as "I'm Every Woman" played in the background. I don't know how but somehow I had made it through Zumba. I grabbed my things and left hurriedly.

I drove around aimlessly for hours, not wanting to confront the information I held in my possession, that my husband was cheating on me.

BOOM, divorce happened. Who would've ever thought?! The next couple of months were completely devastating. The lies, finding out about the other women, the "I'm not happy" conversations, the disrespect... Never in a million years would I think this man, my best friend, my ride or die, the man I would give my life for, would treat me this way. We had been through hell and back TOGETHER and LOVE and an unforsaken God had gotten us through and now you tell me you don't love me anymore, you lie about wanting to be married (only to find out he had another woman). I felt like I was in a twilight zone and wanted to pinch myself to wake up from this nightmare. Was my whole marriage a fraud?

I woke up in a daze. Dust filled the air, my pillows were soaked from crying, and my legs were numb, as I hadn't gotten out of bed in days. Finally, my mom snatched me out of bed and told me I had to pull myself together immediately, that life had to go on. I got up, went into the bathroom, looked in the mirror, and all that I could say was, "Who is this person standing before me?"

This is when I realized that my life had been consumed by other people's wants and needs.

Even as you read the earlier paragraphs, it was all my husband this, my husband that, but what about me?? I had always been the life-saver, the one to solve problems, the one to go overboard to be there for everyone, but did I fight that hard for myself? I had been so extremely consumed with my husband and his situation and HIS happiness that I had forgotten about my own. Alone, distraught, devastated, and confused, I asked myself again, who is the person that stands before me? What are her likes and dislikes? What does she do for fun? Not *we*, but she. I realized that again, it was always *we*, never *she* and somehow, someway, I had to figure out a way to get through this.

My faith, family, and friends really pushed me through. Also, the realization that I am my biggest asset and that no one loves you more than YOU. Take the time to truly understand yourself, who you are, what you like to do, even if you have a family, husband, kids, and/or are consumed by something else. Make sure you know who you are without them because that is really important for growth and self- love. I had tried to find happiness many times through other people, through love and outpouring of compassion. While that is okay, I lost *myself* in those efforts.

There's absolutely nothing wrong with loving your friends, family, husband, etc., however, make sure that you love yourself just as hard in the process.

Take time for yourself on a consistent basis, again, without anyone, so that you don't wake up as I did and say, "*Who am I, who is this person looking back at me in the mirror*??" We should, as women, also give ourselves permission to be okay with making mistakes. It's okay not to be perfect, not to do everything well, and not to be everything for everybody. That's absolutely okay and you are not less of a person because of it. Take those opportunities to have your family and friends be there to support you in those times when you just can't do it all. It doesn't make you any less of a woman that you can't do it all, it just makes you human ☺.

My journey has been quite fulfilling, with twists and turns and still several questions about my passions and career. I still don't have all the answers, but that's okay. This thing called life is a journey. While I do not condone the way that things happened with my now ex-husband, I appreciate the fact that I could leverage the hurt and sadness and begin a new journey with myself. I can begin to love again in a new light and ensure that the next person loving me will do so as unconditionally and as genuinely as I love myself.

I've learned that I have to be a lot of things for myself, self-love. I have to be the thing that I am asking for from my relationships. I went from a complete devastation to a profound revelation. I'm born to succeed, anointed to prosper, blessed beyond measure, and a conqueror... and so are you!

Tnitra King has helped her family celebrate a lot of firsts: she was valedictorian for her graduating class at Beddingfield high school in 1998, and was also a first-generation college student, receiving her Bachelor of Science degree in Computer Science from North Carolina Agricultural and Technical State University in May 2002. During her tenure at North Carolina A&T, she held many leadership positions: president of ACM, president of Society of Women Engineers, and Engineer of the Year, to name a few.

She has also given back to women of divorce on several levels since her own divorce experience.

Tnitra has worked in the IT industry for over sixteen years. Her post-college IT experience has led her to work for many of the Big 5 companies and established financial institutions such as IBM, Wells Fargo, and Bank of America. Her current role is with Wells Fargo as a Technology Manager.

Outside of work, Tnitra enjoys teaching children about Technology and has hosted several workshops on building websites, creating apps, and more. She enjoys buying/selling real estate, travelling, helping others, and spending time with her family and friends.

Stay connected with me on Facebook @ **Job4WhatCEOTnitra**

CHAPTER 3

TWENTY MOVING FORWARD

by Raw Wisdom

I get so caught up in how history repeats itself. I look at my second-oldest daughter from inside and out; most of the time I cry inside as I hear and see her struggle with this thing we all call life. Often my child comes to me to talk about certain things that she is going through. Sad to say most of the time it's when shit has already hit the fan for her.

She is a 20-year-old young black girl (who thinks she is a woman) raised up in the suburbs, but she seems to strive to be great in a place that don't give a fuck about her, and that's the hood. That's right, the hood. Most of us know about the hood because we lived there or live near one and know someone who lives there. Well my daughter used to be so bubbly and when she was in school she made A's, B's, and C's. That child was so smart, but when she was 15 she woke up one day and just seemed to want to learn things the hard way, even though I worked my ass off to make things very easy for my four girls. It has always been me and them. You see, I've been a single mother since day one with all my girls (why?) because I was her, had to be in the hood. See, I was kinda raised in the hood from VA to Philly. When I say kinda, it's because VA's hood wasn't as hood compared to what Philly was dealing with. I didn't understand that until I was forced to go there and live at the age of 14 because of my actions at school one day....

Well, back to my child, she started doing bad in school. Her 9th and 10th grade years were hell for her and me. I was at the school weekly because of her actions. Oh, by the way, she suffers from ADHD, so that's why she couldn't focus. Ok, so we figure that piece out and got her help as far as medicine goes, something I always said I wouldn't do, put my child on when she was younger.

Only if I knew better...being a young mother!!! So, because she couldn't focus in school, she started skipping school with friends and picked up a habit of smoking weed. Yep, that's right, the gateway drug.

This led to her dropping out of school, and this had caused a division between my daughter and me—someone who I vowed to protect, love, shelter, and walk with regardless!!!! Those were my words to my second daughter as I held her in my arms on July 21, 1998, the day after she was born, you know how you just sit and hold your child and look over them to make sure they are just fine in all areas. As of today, my daughter is going through some tough times because of the choices she made. It hurts me because all I see is me but 5x worse and this isn't a good thing. She is definitely me and her father all mixed up into one when I was 20. The only difference is she has no kids. I had two, her sister and her.

So recently she came to me asking, "Mom why is it that every time I try to do good or do one good thing, something bad always happens to me?" And at that moment I had to tell my child all about my past and that place called the hood and that place called the suburbs. Me, Rachel, in my 20's moving forward....

"You see Porsha, I was you, that's why I stay on you. You thought I was picking or you felt like the black sheep out of the 4 girls I had, when that wasn't the case. I see me in you all so clear...you must listen to me as I talk to you right now.... Do you remember me working two jobs and always being tired?" "Yes mommy I do and you were always at work."

"Well you know why, because I wanted to do what I wanted to do when I was your age, so I lacked responsibility. In my 20's all I wanted to do was party, fight and hang out in the hood and do hood shit, from smoking weed, drinking, talking shit, staying up all night with my (friends) so I thought...."

"Believe it or not I was a hustler before I met your father, that's why I didn't see anything wrong with dealing with a hustler, and of course I really didn't have a father to tell me what not to do when it came to certain men and my mother rarely said anything to me as far as men goes. Maybe that was because I was acting like you, grown and thought I knew everything. I was 18 at the time, but before then I was hustling, making money, and yes I smoked weed and sold it. Yep that's right your bougie mom, as you say, was a hustler in her day. One thing about me, I sold my weed first and would worry about smoking later. The things I saw growing up, I learned from. Sometimes you must look at people and learn what not to do instead of looking at them trying to learn what to do!!!!

I always said I will never put my habit in front of my money if I sold any drugs. Was this my plan as a kid? Hell no but, I was always around older folks so that made me seem older than my age. I was the quiet one never spoke too much. I just watched and when shit got real with the drinking and drugging, I took my ass to bed. Sad to say my older friends and family offered me crack, powder cocaine as well as pills, and you know what, before they had a chance to force me to it or offer again I said no and left the room or the whole entire environment. That was a part of growing up that I wasn't ready for."

"I had already fucked up by not finishing school on time, I wasn't about to add to my bad situation. So, while having kids I had to now work 2 jobs and go back to school to further my education because I refused to be stuck working at fast food all my life. My taste of living was too expensive for that shit. As a kid, I always dreamed and thought about living a certain way. It took for me to have 3 kids, no house and a piece of shit ass car that only got me from A to A..."

"Mom, A to A? What is that????"

"I had a car that took me nowhere so I couldn't hold a job and without a job how could I get a house for me and my kids?

I had hit rock bottom this time, it wasn't me by myself it was me with three beautiful kids that didn't ask to be here.... You see my choices! Are you following me??? Meaning are you listening?"

"Mom I don't think your choices was that bad, we are doing fine and so are you..."

"...Are you doing fine Porsha???? (oh) You see Porsha, there you go thinking that wasn't bad, but it was. Look I have three kids by two men that's locked up and because I desired a hustler I am now a single mother and to be honest I'm ok, but my concern is yall. Now my daughters are being raised like I was, a mother struggling to make it without their fathers because they're locked up...look at history, my father your grandfather was locked up all my life damn near. You and Niq's father has been locked up all your life just about. Yes, he was out here and there, but he has done more time in than out. Look where that has you. Maybe if he was here to assist me with you and be your other outlet just maybe things would have turned out a little different."

"I would tell yall that yall fathers are good men/fathers but in reality how good can a father be if he is always absent. How do you have 3 baby daddies and all three are locked up? One has 25 years for a crime he didn't commit.

The hood that he lived in, looked up and out for, and took care of when he was out here, got him 25 years. They lied on him. Diamond's father had life without parole until he fought and fought and got it overturned...but look, he had to spend 18 years in. How old is she, 17. Des' father has been in and out since day one for drugs and other things.... You see how my choices has affected you and your sisters? My choices stop yall from having a father. Don't get it twisted, I didn't put them in there but I chose to have them as my man.... Had I hung outside the hood a little more my choices in men may have been different. Hell, had I focused more on school than partying my struggle wouldn't have been so heavy."

"So you see Porsha, it's all up to us on where we end up. Get off your present and past situation and start moving and working towards your future. Look ahead, not around and back, look forward honey only you can change this. As much as I would love to change things for you, I can't!!! You must love yourself enough to say enough is enough. Also be around people that want to uplift you, not tear you down or put you in a position to be on a standstill. This is what I had to do to become the woman that I am today. I refuse to allow my downfalls and heartaches to make me bitter and a failure at life.... Some don't understand how I made it, why I'm so happy. Even on my bad days I smile and thank God,. You know why? Because it makes me appreciate the good and great days that are ahead.

I refuse to be stuck at the bottom of the barrel. Your life is worth the fight just like mine was. Just know you must learn from your mistakes in order to make it out. Baby girl you're 20 and moving forward. I'm 40 and moving forward, now let's walk our walk." To be continued ...

Raw Wisdom

Allow Raw Wisdom to be your voice of reason! God gave this extraordinary woman the talents to assists others with life skills. After much prayer, Raw's passion and energy birthed a new journey to become an empowering Life Skills Coach.

This highly motivated, family oriented, newly engaged mother of (4) daughters (3)bonus daughters has given herself permission to be spiritually driven and assist others with focusing on their best self. She is the proud CEO of Can We Talk, also known as RAW WISDOM.

Raw's desire has always been to assist others with tapping into the strength that comes from using your **"Mind over Matter"** skills to **"Walk your Walk"**, on this journey called life. Her coaching includes Wellness, Relationship/Intimacy, Recovery, Social Re-Entry, and Family Mediation.

Her clients are empowered with knowing they have a safe and confidential place to vent, have solutions, and guidance offered/provided as needed. Raw's services are one-on-one with undivided attention offering tools to enhance her clients life skills.

Her mission statement is simple: Let me Inform, Impact and Inspire.

Stay connected with me on Facebook @ rachel.webster.984

CHAPTER 4

FIGHT OR FLIGHT

by Salvia Giridhar

There are moments in life that make you question, “What was the purpose of this?” or, “Why am I going through this?” I know at some point you too may have asked yourself this question about one situation or another. I was just like anyone else. I wanted to come out of college, jump straight into the workforce, save up for a house, and chase all the dreams that we are told to work for. Well, my higher power had HIS own plans!

When I was twenty-two, I started having the unfortunate experience of having to contend with a stalker. Now, I know what you're thinking: ex-boyfriend, etc.... Well, no, in this case, it was an OLDER gentleman from church (of all places). It was pure coincidence that my family met him, and it turned into a horrible situation. He would show up at my place of work, at the grocery store, at my gym...he even started progressing to show at the house multiple times. There is not a feeling in the world worse than having to always look over your shoulder. You can only tell someone to go away only so many times before they start to get bold. I remember the number of phone calls, the hanging up, the blocked phone calls, the sound of his voice on the multiple voice mails he would leave, professing his love. I tried so many times to get rid of this guy. I didn't realize how much it had started to take a toll on my stress and my emotions. I remember the panic I became to have when I saw a blocked number on my phone. At first, it was just the calls and nonstop harassment, but it progressed into trespassing. He would show up and just sit on the front porch for extended periods of time, so, of course, this had become a law enforcement/legal matter. I hated having to continually go to the courthouse to file trespassing violations. I hated the endless hours sitting in court to testify every time he was arrested, and the days on end that I had to take off from work. This took so much of my time, my energy, my mental space.

I kept asking, "Why? What do you do to get someone to go away? How does someone get so fixated on another person?"

The climax of almost two years of this harassment hit one Thursday afternoon when I was in the kitchen of my parents' home. If you can picture the layout of the kitchen for a moment...the island faces the living room, to my left was the hallway leading to the foyer, and behind me was the door leading to the basement and formal dining room. I heard a noise on the stairway coming up from the basement. This man had made his way into our home from the basement door, crept upstairs, and entered the kitchen hallway. When I saw him, I immediately grabbed the first thing I could and fought him away from me. There is nothing worse than having to fear for your life. It seemed like a split-second but the last thing I remember was, he was bleeding and left the house. I have no idea how much time this all took. I remember vividly what that fear felt like, I remember my heart racing and trying to calm myself down enough to call the police and my family. This would start a second spiral of court dates that finally ended another year and eight months later.

When you have someone, who has "taken" your sense of peace from you, you desperately do what you can do get it back.

You try to walk around without constantly fearing who may be watching while trying to stop looking over your shoulder every five seconds. To try and "get back" my space, I attempted to do what I as necessary to move on with life because life still has to go on. I finally started to put things back together and moved into my first apartment, which in hindsight may not have been the best idea. I started working in DC, was decorating my new apartment, and had a new puppy, so life started to ***seem normal*** again; however, some things kept lingering. I couldn't figure out why I was having terrible insomnia and why I just wasn't myself. I remember my sudden mood swings, my constant feeling of looking at the world as an outsider versus an active participant. To top of it all off, the first reaction is to pour yourself a drink to "try and relax" and maybe I'll fall asleep.

Depression had set in. All the typical symptoms were there such as: loss of appetite, an inability to focus, withdrawal from social activities or even mundane daily tasks like driving and showering became difficult. It was as though the sun was trying to fight its way in. I was just completely numb and not myself. I was always tired but found it difficult to sleep, and was wracked with guilt, wondering if I was "just being lazy." It's amazing what the body goes through when it has experienced trauma. I spent those first 3 years not understanding what had happened. What many may not know about this emotion is that it's on the opposite spectrum of anger.

When you cannot cope with or have a release for the anger you've felt, it unfortunately manifests itself on the other end and turns inward. It's the lesser of two evils I guess.

Depression isn't a lethargic feeling, it's an active state of pain. One that many people finally give up on by, unfortunately, ending their life. I thought about that myself. Why could I just not get myself in gear? I could be in a conversation with someone, but never REALLY in the conversation. I remember one day in the peak of summertime, I was in my usual state of existence, shades drawn and curled up on the couch. I wanted the world to just go away. It was then that I noticed the curtains, and a small stream of light was trying to force its way through my lovely blackout drapes. But remember, I was still drinking to help myself to sleep which is a vicious cycle! I've just been adding more fuel this fire and was in a nice whirlwind that I'd manifested myself. How do I fix myself? Get angry and Fight.

I finally spoke to my mother and my best friend about what I was experiencing. While stress- related PTSD/depression is new to many people, there is nothing greater than having a support system of loved ones that will push you be better. While many people would suggest medication, my family forced me to get up and move.

They knew how active of a person I had always been and couldn't fathom me not even wanting to leave to go to grocery store, so they were relentless. They kept me active in every definition of the word, even to the point where I started dreading their phone calls or presence at my house.

Slowly but surely, I finally found motivation enough to get back to the gym, but this time I went back to boxing, which is something I hadn't done since college. That first day felt like home again! This was what I needed to force me back to myself. I realized how much I missed the feeling of working harder than your circumstances and your own self-doubt. The fight was with me! My only hurdle was overcoming my own mind. To remind yourself of who you are, what you've overcome and are preparing yourself for is a constant conversation that we all have with ourselves.

Boxing is like life and it literally saved my life. You have your opponent, whatever that may be. It could be related to your career, your external relationships, a trying time in life or even your own self-doubt. Just like in life, you have your "corner." Your support system could be your family, friends, or your faith. At the end of the day, the success is solely dependent on you.

You can run from it, you can hide, you can even drink to avoid that "opponent", but at the end of the day you must stand up and face it. I love that challenge. I know that I'm the one in charge of my own soul, my experience, my mood, and my outcomes.

I was about one year in before I got recertified as a trainer and soon had a steady stream of clients and committed regular members who would show up to my classes. I would always tell my clients that there is nothing I am going to do to them that life won't do, so my goal is to challenge them to be mentally prepared for anything that may come their way. I knew their life stories and could help guide that process. It was those clients that eventually helped me. I realized that the trust they had in me forced me to look at my alcohol dependency and depression differently. I will be stronger for myself so that I can in turn be stronger for other people. That become my calling and what I've been blessed to do. I realized that our experiences are a driving factor in how we change the lives of the people around us. I regret nothing in my life, despite moments where I couldn't physically stand from the mental fatigue.

Life is about fundamentals, boxing is about fundamentals, mental/physical health is about mastering those fundamentals.

The chess match called life does not come with a game plan. It's about repetition and discipline in how we approach the circumstances of our lives. The key is to find ways to be open and understand the energy around you and what you are experiencing. I've found that scars are badges of honor. There is a fighter in each of us and it's through those storms that we realize how much resilience we have inside of ourselves. If you've ever faced a trying period in life you likely have experienced your ability to tap reserves of determination and courage you didn't know you had. The fight or flight response is going to kick in...how will you respond?

"Boxing is like life," Those are the stirring words echoed by Salvia Giridhar; Indian born, personal trainer, boxing coach, and nutritionist. Your "opponent" could be troubles in your career, a relationship, or even your own self-doubt. And in your "corner" could be your family, friends, or faith. You can run, you can hide, but at the end of the day you must stand up and face it! She challenges herself and others around her to remember that we are always in charge of our own soul, experiences, mood, and outcomes.

Salvia proudly earned her Bachelor of Science degree in Business Management from Virginia Polytechnic Institute and State University. She currently puts that degree to work as a Marketing Manager for the Department of Defense for the past eleven years.

This extraordinary transformer trains clients in weight-loss, increased muscle-tone, and nutrition. She also works with competitive athletes on speed, increased muscle performance, and balance. Sports include boxing, track and field, soccer, and dance. Not only does she take joy in working with their exterior makeover for her clients, she works harder on their interior makeover. Salvia understands the fight in life can be tough. She wants people to remember that there is always beauty in the storm and who we become once that storm passes.

Aside from all her passion and seriousness, one of the many things that makes Salvia smile is...a good hair day and some cute shoes!

Stay connected with me on Facebook @ salvia.giridhar

CHAPTER 5

FIFTY THREE SHADES OF GREEN

by Lorie P. Woodruff

Four thirty nine, forty seven sixty, and one zero one. Four thirty nine, forty seven sixty, and one zero one. $4.39, $47.60, and $1.01. It was a chilly February morning in 2012, I'm sitting on the side of my bed, and those were the three bank balances I saw, as I scrolled through my bank app on my phone. How in the hell did I get here?

I'm supposed to be in a perfect relationship. I'm supposed to be a top realtor at my real estate office.

I'm supposed to have the most generous friends. I'm supposed to have money in the bank. Right? If I knew what I know now, these silly expectations would have never come in my mind in the first place.

Prior to 2012, I lived in a world of "glamour". Money was not a major problem, my career was exciting, my relationships were plentiful, family ties were strong, and my love life was looking hopeful. I never sought out to be the popular girl but my natural energy could not resist being around people. It seemed like a party was going on every weekend and I had to be there. Traveling, new restaurants, new home, new church home, new experiences, and more. My man and I were like Jay Z and Beyonce. That's who I thought was going to be my last date, in life. Mistake number one.

As time moved on, I began feeling disconnected from myself. I thought it was something a pill could fix because I heard that kids with ADD (Attention Deficit Disorder) popped a pill and their focus was illuminated. I needed that! My job started feeling like work, my relationships started getting distance, and I began accusing my man of anything and everything. Why was I getting on my own nerves? I couldn't stand the person I was becoming and I found myself crying more and more.

I made a phone call to a local doctor who could get me the prescription, that I was so anxious for.

I met him at his office and was ready for my "focus prescription". The psychiatrist barely listened to me for thirty minutes and he scribbled on a piece of paper. Now we are getting somewhere, I thought to myself! I took the prescription and excitedly walked to my car. I sat in the car and just looked at the "focus prescription" and then my phone rang. Why was my sister calling me in the middle of the day? She never calls me during this time. She's a school teacher and this was odd to me. She asked me where I was and she quickly told me, "do not fill that prescription". I laughed and let her know I was going to do it anyway. I needed something to help me focus and I had the solution in my hand. She repeatedly told me not to fill the prescription. I told her ok, just to get her off the phone. No more than ten minutes later, our mother called. What in the world, I thought. She also told me not to fill that prescription, as it could alter my mind. Now, I'm crying in the car and feeling even more sad. What now? What is supposed to help me? What was supposed to be an easy afternoon of getting a simple prescription, now turned into some intervention between my sister and mom. Little did I know, God was reaching around the situation. My spiritual ignorance never thought about asking God what to do. Mistake number two.

I filled that "focus prescription". It was only five dollars, thanks to my health insurance. The devil sure has a way of luring you closer to him. I never took the pills but I kept them just in case I felt weak. Mistake number three.

It's now winter 2012. This particular morning, I woke up to $53 in my account, so how was this day really going to work out? I was invited by a close friend to go Downtown to a women's conference. He knew I was walking in confusion and he had the perfect place for me to go. Crying every day became a normal act for me, so I jumped out on trust and went. I had never gone to an event by myself and felt so welcomed by everyone. The speaker was Bob Yates and their entire focus was on building women up from the inside out. It didn't matter what each woman looked like on the outside, we started peeling back layers that made each of us feel good. This was unfamiliar but I welcomed it! I was lead to purchase one of the speakers books. I had never purchased books that were intended for therapy. I supported others in the past and some of those books sat comfortably on my book shelf. It was something different about this day. As the author, Melanie Bonita, signed my book, I felt happiness peak through. Could this book be the "focus prescription" I needed all along? Was God putting me in position to get out of this funk?

The book was now in my home. I opened the book like it was Christmas day. Every morning and night, I would read a page. Each page was filled with an affirmation and positive quote for the day. Yes, I needed my "new focus prescription" in the morning and at night. It was that bad. From there, I would post on Facebook the positive quotes from that particular day. Wow, I'm feeling better and amazingly my online friends needed it too. Could others be looking for this "new focus prescription" I had my hands on? As a result of this newfound prescription, I'm waking up before 10am; I'm waking up with a smile and going to bed in peace; I'm smiling during the day for no reason; I'm single; I'm alive. I'm happy!

You wonder how does someone get to that point in life. Life lessons will come unannounced and without warning. I had to be very honest and quiet with myself and figure some things out. Clearly, I was not on a healthy path and even reality TV didn't show this kind of episode I was staring in. Depression was never what I wanted to label it but that is what "they" call it when your mind needs a reset and you feel sad. Society puts so many labels around the disorder that it never gives us a fair opportunity to defend it. We are the directors of our lives and if we don't learn to be grateful for what and who we have, God will step in and disrupt life for however long he wants.

You're thinking now. She had a lot of things going for her, what gets someone to that point of happy and then sad? I'm not sure I can even admit that I was truly happy. Sure, I was content but not enthusiastically happy with life. The expectations of life began to settle in and when they weren't met or exceeded, I did not know how to handle it. My personal relationship suffered and later dissolved because I was not in a happy place in life. It's sad to know when you are going through a rough episode in life, no one can understand you or relate. They just leave. Now you must pick yourself up and deal with more sadness on top of sadness. My work life had begun to decline because I just didn't feel motivated any more. I still worked but put on the performance of a lifetime to hide the pain that was going on backstage.

The "new focus prescription" book lead me to go on a journey of personal development. 2012 was the year a new Lorie was born. I got introduced to more positive association groups, started reading more inspirational books and began watching motivational men and women speak on stages across the United States. A new life means purging the old way of thinking to building a new belief muscle inside of me. Daily action had to be taken to master this disaster in my mind.

While in flight one day to a conference, I was encouraged to write a book and I got so far as to write the title on a Delta napkin and leave it alone. I had no idea of chapter content or even how the book was to be sold. Step one was done. The idea was born and then I created the book title. Winter of 2012 was the year my first book titled *Unleash Your Irresistibility: Secrets To Making Every Man Want You* was born. I would look at the title I created on a Delta napkin for years before I decided to move forward and publish it in 2016. Timing had to be right to help mold me mentally, spiritually, and financially to began that journey. Lessons had to be learned and new experiences had to be achieved to make the book a better success.

No matter what is going on backstage in your life, there will always be moments that we are ashamed of or don't publicly give praise. 2012 was the beginning of a turning point for me. No one can accomplish their "new" self in 30 days or less, this takes years to master the process of development. The lessons I learned came hard and they came with an assignment for others.

The first lesson I learned was that it's ok to live in expectation but you must put God first, you second, and man last. My days were spent putting man/money/friends first, myself second, and God last.

This was a disaster waiting to happen. Your well being and connection have to come from God so that you can handle life. Prior to 2012, episodes of jealousy, fear, doubt, and insecurity ran high with me. Why? Because my life was not in proper order. Had I taken the "focus prescription" from the doctor, I may not be here today in my right mind. You can't artificially alter your mind when God has already given us what is necessary to live an abundant life. We just have to work that belief muscle and keep going and going. The "new focus prescription" was the perfect medicine that I needed to survive and be a blessing to someone else. I thank God everyday for meeting Melanie Bonita because she was the angel sent to give hope to myself and others. Melanie's book cost me $15, the doctor's prescription was $5, and at that time in 2012, I had $53 to my name. I will eternally invest money in myself, by way of education, in order to live the best life I can and bring others to their best life also. If you only focus on the cheap price tag, your life, your family, and your dreams could suffer from one cheap and weak moment.

The second lesson I learned was that you must remain thankful and grateful. Some people will come into your life out of nowhere to bless you or block you. You have to be totally connected to God in order to understand this discernment. Prior to 2012, I never thanked God for all that I had or didn't have.

I just figured, I worked for it and voila, here are my rewards. Wrong! From the time you wake up in the morning to the time you close your eyes at night, constant thanks and gratitude must happen.

My third lesson was recognizing when to let toxic situations go. The worst gift in the world could be wrapped up in a beautiful bow, called friends or family. We think it all looks great on the outside but they are truly there to take something from us. Your energy has to be at a high level at all times in order to be in tuned with removing the wrong people or situations out of our lives. You will gain a sense of peace once this is done and you can begin to vibrate and elevate the way God's needs you to.

My story is still being written, as is yours. There will always be peaks and valleys in your life. The secret is knowing how to use your God given power to create your life. We have the power, we just have to keep it and not give it away to others. 2012 was my turning point and I vowed to stay as far away from fifty three dollars as I can. It's time to unleash and get more shades of green!

Rock stars come in many varieties, and not all of them have a thing to do with music. Lorie Woodruff is one such individual, and if you are not careful, she will most likely have created another entrepreneurial symphony by the time you finish reading this. Her personal drive and ambition are typically on full throttle and she is determined to let nothing stand in her way of success. She has proven this time and again and will continue to do so while simultaneously inspiring others to greatness along the way. Her only question to you is "Are you ready to upgrade your lifestyle by saying 'yes' to yourself"?

In the past several years, this multitalented real estate extraordinaire, author of Unleash Your Irresistibility: Secrets To Making Every Man Want You, international speaker, and host of Lorie TV has garnered some major hits, proving she is far from a one-hit wonder. This entrepreneurial rock star has appeared on TV One with Roland Martin and several radio shows, discussing credit makeover techniques; cover girl and featured in HerLife magazine, a magazine featuring inspirational women entrepreneurs; she has won numerous awards for top sales and performance in real estate sales and network marketing; has presented countless seminars on personal growth, real estate, credit repair and business opportunities, changing the lives of individuals and offering them advice on ways to earn extra streams of income through network marketing; and she established herself as a team leader for Novae, a personal growth and self development company of which she had helped catapult in the Maryland and Washington, DC area. By all accounts, Lorie will continue to top the charts with unparalleled accomplishments, not just to increase her income and personal goals, but also with the direct objective of helping as many other people as she can along the way. Lorie is not just a party of one when it comes to embracing success on all levels. She extends an invitation to succeed to everyone, and will gladly assist on the journey.

A long-standing presence within the real estate industry, Lorie was raised in the Washington DC area. She always had a strong work ethic within herself. She was nourished by the entrepreneurial spirit of her parents and used that sustenance to fuel her ambitions. By keeping true to her silly, playful, and tell it like it is nature, she continues to break the traditional molds of female entrepreneurs.

Stay connected with me on Facebook @ hostoflorietv

CHAPTER 6

OWN IT. BE YOU

by Nicole Welton

Life itself has many events, good and bad, that has always taken place. Whether you're in a very prosperous situation, whether you're in a very bad situation, whether you're just sitting here in life trying to figure out what is next, after reading this chapter you will know what is next.

I am 27 years-old and am currently a full-time employee and a part time entrepreneur, in hopes of retiring my job in January of 2019. The thing that I love about creative power is that we all possess it, we all have it, and this is something that I truly did not even understand just a year ago. I didn't understand that everything that I wanted, I already had access to it, but it's up to me to be able to bring it into the physical world.

I reflect back on being a child. I was very insecure, I was small, and I was under 100 pounds until I got into ninth grade. I was often picked on and laughed at, and often misunderstood, and it trickled into my adult life because I didn't have that confidence, I didn't have that self-esteem. Because I was battling with who I was, who Nicole Welton really was, it gave me different bad experiences within my relationships, within my friendships, and I could not understand why I was experiencing that disconnect. But I had to go through those tough experiences and learn those lessons in order to truly blossom into the woman that God wanted me to be.

I remember very vividly being 24 years-old and still being so lost and confused and feeling like the only thing that would make me happy was someone else's validation.

I thought that the only way I would be able to succeed in life was through a handshake and a congratulations and a pat on the back from someone else. I thought that that was it, I thought that in order to know that I really did a good job, somebody has to tell me I did a good job! That was such a problem for me because that's what I always was looking for, but I didn't really receive it. So, it all stems back to when you choose your partner, when you choose your friends, you're choosing these people based off of a reflection of where you are in your life. And because of where I was in my life, I was not in good relationships. I was not in the best of friendships, just because of where I was in my life.

Then I sat down December 4th, 2017 and really looked in the mirror, and asked, "Who is Nicole Welton? What does she have to offer the world? What is her purpose?" I was crying out for help, I was so emotional and I was looking for answers, I was looking for healing, because I was tired of being in a state of blaming other people for how my life was. I was tired of being in a state of constantly wanting validation, constantly wanting acceptance, constantly wanting attention, constantly wanting to be recognized just for what I was doing. I was in that state, and it was so draining. I was in a state of insecurity, and as a woman if you do not tackle your insecurity and understand that you're beautiful just the way that God made you, it can be a hindrance.

I would literally shrink in a room filled with other women. I was not confident to be in a room with other beautiful women because I felt I was not as beautiful as them. I didn't have the gifts that they had. I didn't possess the talents that they had. And I would shrink because I was insecure. I would shrink if I thought my significant other was even looking at another woman. Why? Because I thought maybe he wants her over me. These are real situations, and these are real feelings and emotions that I know many people will experience in life. I don't think it's something that is avoidable, but you'll have to be able to recognize the lesson in it. And that's what I had to sit down with and really sit in.

So, on December 4th, 2017, that was the day that really started to be a major shift for me in my life, because I had to build my relationship with God, I had to understand, "Okay God, you put me on this earth for a reason and for a purpose. Nothing in your name is of lack, nothing in your name is of missing of anything. You put me here for a reason. I sat down looking in my mirror and I kept crying and crying and crying and crying. And I wrote down all of the traits that I wanted to get rid of. I wanted to get rid of insecurity, I wanted to get rid of hate, I wanted to get rid of jealousy, I wanted to get rid of envy, and I wanted to get rid of just overall not being a happy soul. These are the traits I wrote down on an index card and placed in my prayer box.

And I prayed over this. I said, "Lord, please withdraw these traits from me. Please withdraw these characteristics from me. Lord, please withdraw anything of lack from me, from my heart, from my spirit." And I prayed on this, and as I'm praying, I'm still just crying. I'm just crying, and I didn't have anyone there to say, "What's wrong?" but I didn't need anyone there at this moment to say "What's wrong?" because as I continued to sit in silence, that's when I heard God's voice so loud and so clear, and he said, "Nicole, this is your breakthrough. You have to commit to doing the work on yourself and everything that you ever wanted in life will begin to fall into place and into alignment."

And that is what I want to speak on. You have to commit to doing the work on yourself. So many people try to give people advice, and we don't give ourselves advice. We give people some of the best advice, and we don't even take that advice for ourselves. You have to do the work first, you have to heal first, you have to understand and be complete and whole in yourself first. You have to do this first! Once you do this, and once you truly heal, and once you truly come out of your mess, you are able to bless people with what your story is, with what your testimony is, because you've come out of that mess. But you cannot give people advice when you are still in your hurt, while you are still in your healing process.

And I thank God for everything that I went through, all the traumatic experiences as a child, as a young adult, even as an adult. I thank him, I thank God for those struggles, and I thank God for putting me in those situations and putting me to the test, because I aced the test. I aced the test! So be grateful that you were chosen to go through that struggle. Be grateful that you were chosen to go through that battle. Why? The lesson on the other side is so much of a greater reward, you'll have such a feeling and a peace of being that is out of this world! God is so magnificent! He is so magnificent in everything that he does.

And I plead with you, after you read this chapter, sit! Sit in a room in a silent space with index cards and look at yourself in the mirror, and pray to God to get rid of all the characteristics that you want him to withdraw from your life. Pray on that, write those things out, see it, and say it out loud, over and over again: "Lord, this is done. I'm so glad that all of these characteristics are removed from my life. Thank you so much that you have removed this from my life, thank you so much that I am in transition of being a complete and happy soul. Thank you so much that I am in transition of being a complete and happy person, just from your name, Lord, just from your touching.

Not that anybody else has to give me a validation, not that anybody else has to give me a recognition, not that anybody else has to tell me, "Good job," because why, God, you told me "Good job." You told me "Good job."

Sit in it. Pray. Write. And pray over it. And begin the healing. The takeaway point for this chapter is to heal. In order to access, everything of abundance that God has for you, you have to heal. You have to heal! Take a moment for yourself and begin healing. And you're going to feel so vibrant, you're going to feel so alive, you're going to feel so anew. You're going to feel so anew because you took the opportunity to heal. Own your mess. Own your life. Own the good things that have happened, own the things that will happen, own your future, own your present, own your past. Own it! And be you.

Nicole Welton believes in living a life of peace of being and abundance—after you do the hard work on yourself to heal! Nicole was born and raised in Columbia, South Carolina, to her loving parents, Nichelle Welton and Leroy Draft, as well as her "amazing grandmother," Sara Belton. She is currently an activist in her community, providing an avenue for women and men to build generational wealth. She currently transforms the world as a Motivational Speaker, Financial Leadership Coach and CEO of PrettyGirlsTrade, LLC.

Nicole's passion lies in helping people discover what they already have access to within themselves. Her mission is to build an international platform to give people a voice and help them live the life of their dreams.

She has already helped a multitude of women and men discover their life and financial purpose and start their journey to creating their extraordinary legacy.

It makes Nicole smile to see other people prosper and win in life, and it makes her cry to see people suffer and mentally live in poverty. Her motto comes from Oprah Winfrey: "Forgiveness is giving up the hope that the past could have been any different."

Stay connected with me on Facebook @ **NicoleNWelton**

CHAPTER 7

Keep Your Success In Front Of You

by Kita Holmes

My move to Maryland on April 1, 2013 was quite the experience. The move had to be made, yet was very nerve-wracking, because I'd never lived anywhere for 36 years but North Carolina. A book I read that changed my life was, *Who Moved My Cheese*.

This book *was* my motivation to make the transition to the Greater DC area, get out here in this maze called life, and look for new cheese.

I was a real estate broker/owner-operator in North Carolina and my business went belly up. The move was necessary, but I had to keep the success in front of me.

I am a very success-driven person who has seen a lot, been through more than the average person, and I deem there's no obstacle or situation I can't bounce back from fast. My favorite saying is that I'm like a cat and no matter how far you throw me, I'm going to always land on my feet. Consequently, GOD allowed many things to happen before and after this transition to test my faith in that lifelong principle I live by.

I moved to the DC area and landed a lucrative Senior Property Management position that allowed me to use all my leadership skills. I passed the real estate exam for the state of Maryland with flying colors and was ready to pursue my new career. I was hired to direct and oversee a property management division with one of the fastest growing companies in Carroll County. The CEO's vision was to expand her business into Baltimore City/County and ramp up the division quickly. My significant-other was from North Carolina as well and we had hopes to succeed in our relationship; me to become a successful realtor/property manager, and for both of us to enjoy the area together.

He was in the Navy for over 20 years, soon to retire, and we had plans - so I thought. GOD laughs at our plans. He had only one year left in the military, so he enrolled in real estate school to be able to help me, in hopes we would work together. For a year prior to my move, we had a long-distance relationship, talking daily and seeing each other on the weekends. Many people don't agree, but I'm a believer in cohabitation before marriage. When you move in with someone, you see the entire real person who can hide behind dating or weekend visits or scattered visits. As a matter of fact, I saw and learned something entirely different from those sporadic visits once I moved in and relocated.

The first change I noticed was the excessive drinking and alcohol abuse. I saw the isolation and depression setting in from him about to retire from something he did for 20 years. Arguments grew more and more intense. When we argued he would literally disappear and disconnect from me, and act as if I never existed. This was very hard for me because I was alone in a strange area, with one family member who was more than an hour away. I had my work family, and my 15-year-old son, who had relocated with me. My daughter stayed back in North Carolina to finish high school. Talk about lonely!! I think I cried daily and went home every weekend.

My friends and family would ask me, "Did you really move??" My job was great: I was growing the company and was succeeding, but my relationship was VERY dysfunctional. My move and my succeeding at work were very important, so I channeled the pain from a horrible relationship into my work and kept the success in front of me.

In life, we all have triggers and levels of intolerance that will cause us to say things we don't mean. Those feelings and actions usually come from fear, insecurity, and rejection—well, those were my characteristics. Hell, so much so that my success was not in front of me after one argument, and I blew it. That one night we had a huge argument and he tried to disappear, and all I could think about was the rejection of him leaving and disappearing. I said, "Not tonight!!" I shouted, "You won't leave and if you do - you won't leave in that truck. I'm going outside to slash your tires." I went in the kitchen and grabbed a knife to pretend to go slash the tires, and then walked outside. Little did I know, I just needed the air to calm down and the walk to realize what I'd said - that it was all shenanigans. I wasn't going to slash his tires at all. I'm really not that type of person. What I wanted him to do was come running after me and say, "Baby I'm sorry, I'm not going to leave, let's work this out." I wanted the threat to produce another reaction.

Sometimes, you really say one thing in hopes of getting a different response. However, by the time I walked back into the house—yes, my boyfriend had called the police. Once the police arrived they waited as he gathered his things so he could disappear as usual for the night. I didn't mean what I said; I just wanted him to stay. I was crushed - did he really believe I would slash his tires? Never would I. However, this night taught me a valuable lesson. Don't communicate threats while angry in an argument, practice silence; it's the best attribute one can possess in a time of a fight-or-flight situation -if you're truly not in harm's way. It's called SELF CONTROL. A person who can control your emotions, controls you! A successful person, in the heat of anger, can throw it all away in just 30 seconds of not having self control. We've seen this in the media, and, all too many times, these out-of-control actions from celebrities. Do you remember the elevator scene of the NFL football player punching his wife and losing his whole career by that one night of being angry with his significant other? This night, by making that threat, my success was clearly not in front of me. Meanwhile, my boyfriend stayed out all night, and the next morning I was awakened by knocks at the door. I answered the door, and there, standing before me, were two police officers. In my mind, they were coming to check on me from the argument we'd had the night before.

My son was off to school and I was just about to get up and get ready for a mammogram. I said, "Hello," and the police said, "How are you? Are you alright?" I said, "Yes, my boyfriend and I just had a huge argument and he left but I'm ok now. Thanks for checking on me." They stated, "Ma'am, we are not here to check on you." Instead, they handed me a piece of paper that I read. I almost dropped to the ground when I read "Stay away Order." This man filed a protective stay away order that he was able to get a judge to sign off on! The order he wrote said that I had become belligerent in his home and that I threatened him with a knife and that I was going to slash his tires. He pretty much fabricated a lot of it. I was blown away! The officers said, "You have to get your personal belongings now and leave. Get what you need and go." I said, "I can't come back." They said "NO, you can come back if you call a police officer to help you get some things." They stated, "You can't contact him, or come in any close proximity to him." My eyes welled with tears, but I couldn't cry. I quickly gathered my things - I was glad my son had already caught the bus for school - and I left. I was working from home that day. I had a doctor's appointment that I couldn't miss because I had a lump in my breast prior that was benign and I was getting my yearly exam to make sure I had no cancer. After my doctor's appointment, I sat in my car and cried.

Would I get a hotel, or do I just leave and go back home to North Carolina? Where will my son go -- he's in high school with only a month and a half left before the school year is out. I can't possibly take him out of school and send him back home to North Carolina; I can't lose my great job I just got here. What was I going to do? I had attended a church in the area and met some VERY good people. It was a military town, so I met a young lady whose husband was on his last tour out of the country. We had exchanged phone numbers one day after church. I literally was all alone in this city and state. I had no choice: I dialed her number, shaking. I had to keep the success in front me; I could not fail; I could not go back home; I was starting a new life and a new career. I began to tell her my story and she was shocked, but said the words I needed to hear: "You can stay with me until you figure this out." This woman lived literally across the street from where I was living with my boyfriend. It was one room, one bed, and one bathroom that my son and I shared. You talk about character building and humility! However, I refused to fail, and my success was in front of me, not the circumstance or the boyfriend. My success and what I needed to do for me and my family. GOD was with me and I prayed to no end for strength.

The court date came for the protective order. My boyfriend kept his same story as he looked me in the face in the courtroom.

The judge granted him the petition. I tried to explain, “I just paid rent there; I live there; I have food there. The judge didn’t care. She said, “If you-all came to this point, you need to leave.” I left that courtroom, rushed to my car, laid my head on the steering wheel, and finally got that one good cry I needed. I think I cried alone, for 45 minutes. I then pulled myself together and drove to work and pushed through that pain.

About three weeks later the boyfriend called for me to come back, said he was SO sorry, my son needed to finish school comfortably, and that he was going to drop all charges. I needed to get my son and me out of the same bed. I dropped my pride and anger for my son’s and my success, but I had a plan. I went back to his home, allowing my son to finish school, and as soon as the school year was over I moved to Bethesda, Maryland. I got a very nice place, in an awesome school district for my son, and peace of mind for me. During the last few months of me staying with my boyfriend, he asked to me to marry him...yes he proposed! He gave me a ring from Jared and kept trying to make it up to me for what he did. It was too late. I returned the ring and never looked back; I felt he had tried to ruin me. He thought I was going to crumble and move back to North Carolina. He didn’t care about my son, my dreams or my success, but I kept the mission and goals in front of me.

I realized - I did wrong by communicating a threat, but there were no actions behind my threat. Consequently, I learned that in the thick of things you have to keep the bigger picture in front of you, have self control, don't say things you really don't mean, and keep your eyes on your goals and the passion you have for success.

Since my move and tragic episode, my life has changed drastically. I went to therapy, met new friends, and gained new relationships and business acquaintances. I put GOD first; myself, my kids, and my career next, in that order. I am now a business-owner again of one of the fastest growing property management firms, *5 Star Property Management, Inc.* 5 is God's number of grace and his grace was sufficient for me to keep going. He gave me tenacity, perseverance, faith, resilience, and passion - 5 power principles to keep my success in front of me.

A passion for people, a love of the community, and a desire to help make dreams come true, inspired Kita Holmes to pursue real estate. This North Carolina native is no stranger to hard work in the real estate industry and has a twelve year track record to prove it. This ambitious real estate entrepreneur was recognized and awarded "Rookie of the Year" during her first year in real estate. In her second year, Kita's charisma and determination were rewarded with the title "Sterling Society Member," and gained her recognition for quality customer service. After a successful two years, Kita decided to start a boutique real estate firm and further pursued her real estate broker license.

Currently, Kita is an educator, mentor, and President of 5 Star Property Management, servicing Maryland and District of Columbia. Its management style tailors the need of the real estate investor client for efficient passive income. Over the years, her experiences have allowed her to utilize all of her leadership qualities and management skills to help grow and maintain a winning team.

Kita is an active mother of two college-age children. She enjoys spending quality time with family and friends, traveling, and giving to charity.

Stay connected with me on Facebook @ kita.holmes.14

CHAPTER 8

STORMS DON'T LAST FOREVER

by Shakeita Price

"Life is a journey and through every obstacle strength is gained to become better than you were yesterday"- Kendrea Moore

The saying, "Don't judge a book by its cover" is so true; however, people still do, so it is very important to make good first impressions.

It took me a while to learn that. In the process, I learned that I had to change.

As a young child I always made straight A's, but my behavior and attitude always resulted in me getting into trouble. Once I got into high school, I wanted to do my own thing and no longer listened to my elders. My junior year of high school, I concluded that I was going to drop out. Some days, I would not go to school and the days that I did, I arrived late. That year, I failed my English Honors and my Statistics class, and I honestly did not care. Somehow, I returned to school my senior year and worked two jobs with hopes of my boyfriend and I moving together and starting a family. I had no desire to go off to college; my plan was to go to a technical school in the area. All that changed when my boyfriend had a baby with another girl. I really lost myself to the point where I chased him down in the girl's car. Sadly, she slammed on brakes which resulted in my car colliding into hers. Later, this same girl and I got into a physical altercation. The relationship became so toxic for me that I wanted out. Leaving him might have been one of the best things that happened to me at this point in my life, because this was when I became desperate to go off to college. I just wanted to get away from what had broken me and start a new life. I started college that following August after I graduated in May.

When I started college at Coastal Carolina University, I was a wild young lady. I can remember jumping in and out of random cars with my friends, catching rides to room-gatherings and college parties.

I wore very revealing clothes and I was loud and obnoxious. One thing I can say is that God was always present in my life during college, because I never allowed myself to act out to the extent that I had sex with multiple or random people. I was pretty much that girl who would act wild but would never actually give herself up to any and every guy. I decided to join an organization called Leadership Challenge, which changed my life. This organization helped me realize that the way I dressed and presented myself was not lady-like. It taught me leadership skills and how to communicate effectively with others. I was a member for four consecutive years, and so grateful that I was able to make connections with good people who could mentor me.

My sophomore year of college, I joined the Army National Guard. I gave up two consecutive summers to complete my basic training and job training so that I would not miss a semester of school. Even though the isolation from my family and friends was difficult during training, it was one of the best things that had ever happened to me.

The military really broke me down. Entering the military, I had no discipline, no integrity, and a bad attitude. Being ordered around for 3 months and forced to do things that I did not want to do changed me for the better. Even though I was told by one of the drill sergeants that my mother should have aborted me, the training still molded me into a better individual.

When I completed training, I left with discipline and integrity. The military also had great benefits, which helped me get through college without taking out as many student loans.

My junior year of college, I had the opportunity to join a mentoring program where I discovered a passion for working with young girls. I graduated in 2014 and moved back home and founded my nonprofit organization, “Ladies Divine To Shine” for girls between the ages of 12 and 18. The organization utilizes adult volunteers to offer one-on-one mentoring, promote higher education, and increase girls’ self-awareness. The organization continues to grow today.

Also, in 2014, I started graduate school, pursuing counseling which I changed to Social Work in 2016. I sat out of graduate school the year of 2015 when I became pregnant with my daughter and went back the following year after she was born.

I was a single mother but was blessed to have family support from my family and my daughter's father family. However, there were several nights my daughter would wake up and I had to care for her while still having to drive an hour and a half to school the next morning. The two-year journey was definitely hard but I graduated with a 3.9 GPA in May 2018 and passed the Masters Licensed Exam for Social Work in July 2018.

The Social Work Program changed my life in so many ways, and I am forever grateful that the program motivated me to work on myself inside and out. This program made me become more self-aware and face the biases that I had about people.

Nine years ago, I was a homeless, disturbed, lost young lady and had no desire to accomplish the goals that I have accomplished thus far. Today, I am a Licensed Master Social Worker, Veteran of the United States Armed Forces, Founder of a mentoring program, author, great mother, and most importantly, an authentic woman with a genuine spirit and a desire to help others. There is always a constant reminder to share with other women that storms don't last forever.

Shakeita Price is a native of Lamar, South Carolina. She graduated as an honor student from Wilson High School in May 2010. She obtained her Bachelor's degree in Political Science from Coastal Carolina University in May 2014. After obtaining her Bachelor's degree, Ms. Price furthered her education and pursued her Master's degree in Social Work. She graduated from the University of South Carolina May of 2018. Ms. Price is a Licensed Masters Social Worker and is currently employed as a Psychiatric Care Manager in an inpatient hospital. She is also a Veteran of the United States Armed Forces.

In 2014, her passion for youth motivated her to found her nonprofit organization, "Ladies Divine To Shine", which is a mentoring program that offers guidance for girls between the ages of 12 and 18. Her daughter, Amina, is her heartbeat and her primary reason why she keeps moving forward. This master motivator enjoys working out, volunteering in the community, and reading inspirational and self-development books.

Her ultimate goal is to provide young women and girls with the blueprint for reaching their goals and bettering themselves. She plans to launch an inspirational podcast providing young girls with the knowledge she wished she'd had when she was their age!

Stay connected with me on Facebook @ AuthorSPrice-818253481899085/

CHAPTER 9

LOST IN MY TRUTH

by Jackie M. Brooks

Have you ever met someone, who just stopped you in your tracks? I did. Here's my story.

It was a warm July afternoon. Saturday to be exact, in Washington, DC, I had on all white shorts and a backless top. I parked on H street and was getting ready to walk to the Marriott for a day party, when this guy got out his car, as I was paying the meter.

I was blinded by muscles, chocolate and his shiny smooth bald head. OMG, I was already smiling, and his smile was contagious which caused me to smile even more. We exchanged numbers and decided to keep in touch. As the days passed, we communicated more and started hanging out on a regular basis. We had some things in common from being Greek, Mason/Eastern Star, a love for football, bowling and traveling. The more we talked and spent time together, evolved into us being in a relationship together. I began to think, "can this be, true love, the one for me?" As time progressed we began planning a future together.

Ask and it shall be given...

When you are a giver by nature, you give unconditionally and unconsciously not thinking that someone's agenda is not pure. He asked, I gave. The sky was the limit from an apartment, furniture, cell phone, and even a truck. I told him "no" several times, but was quilted in doing so, because he started saying, "what you won't do another woman will". I allowed him to get in my head. How are you going to let another woman do for your man? So, I gave of myself, time and finances unselfishly, thinking I was doing something for us, but it was for selfish gain.

Something, Something, Something, Just Ain't Right...

When we first met and began to hang out, I asked the normal questions, that everyone asks when getting to know a person: Age, kids, married, divorced, parents living or deceased, siblings, what you do, gay/bisexual/straight, where you live, likes and dislikes and goals? As months went by, things just weren't adding up. He even said he was a NFL ex-player - yeah right! Funds were constantly tied up. Damn! No money for gas or to get something to eat! I began asking questions, that weren't being answered or the answers just didn't make sense, which caused me to start thinking, *this man is lying*. The more he asked me to do this and that, the more his shi$ just didn't add up. The truth or lies will all be revealed in due time.

I Can't Believe It...

I have spent over $10,000 in less than a year! My credit is now f@#$%^ up just from being nice, trusting and too damn giving. I am just one who trusts others until given a reason not to. This comes from being raised according to the Golden Rule: Do unto others, as you would have them do unto you. I just didn't believe there were people out there who didn't live like this, but apparently there are.

Losing Myself...

By now, I was totally confused and disappointed. How could this be happening to me? I was beating myself up, not eating, and couldn't sleep; my hair was coming out. I was completely stressed out, depressed, angry, bitter and frustrated. I was losing control of myself, my finances, and almost lost my mind. My life was spiraling out of control and I didn't know how to reel myself back in but I knew I had to get control because I was having thoughts and visualizations of killing this man. I mean I planned his death out to the tee. Hatred was so heavy on me, I felt that I could have snapped at any moment. Yet, I was still connected to the GOD within me and constantly repented and ask God to remove those thoughts from me. I became disengaged socially from my family and friends, I was embarrassed and didn't want them to know I had f@#$%^ up. Yet, we were still in this relationship because I still wanted to believe he was going to do right and fix it all. I was believing that he loved me and that this was all a dream. My prayers were simple "God, let him do right by me."

Intervention...Help Needed...

I didn't ask for help but my best friends Kera and Rodney reached out to my mom stating they were extremely concerned and wanted to help me get through this. My mom was already concerned for my well-being.

She was asking my sister what was going on, my sister was concerned and just wanted me out of the relationship, by any means necessary. Yet, I didn't know how to get out without being damaged goods. I was going to church listening to Pastor Jenkins do his series on Money Management and just felt so stupid. Here I knew better. I was always taught to never lend money or cosign for anyone, yet I did, believing we were planning our future.

Have you ever wanted help, but didn't want to ask for help? My mom constantly asked "what was going on"? I always replied "nothing, I'm okay." My mother was persistent and determined to help me, for I was her child, her first born. She constantly asked "what can she do and who can she call?" One day, I was crying uncontrollably, I broke down and told her everything. Again, I wasn't asking for help, but my mom was willing to help by any means necessary. My mom helped me abandon that relationship to keep me from losing my mind and total self.

She stepped in and I am forever grateful. I started praying: "*Dear God, help me break away from things and people that are breaking me.*" At this moment, the plan of reclaiming my life was starting.

Enough is Enough...

When you get to a point of being 'sick and tired' of the lies, deception, empty promises you take matters into your own hands. Although in my mind, that relationship had sank, I still had to act as-if we were still in a relationship until I got my truck back. So, I ordered a tracking device (by any means necessary) called him to pick me up from work because I wasn't feeling well. Two things were always true, when I would see him: he would need gas money and was always hungry. Just a user, never have money for anything, yet he had money for rims on the truck. Sure 'nuff, we stopped to get gas, he asked me for $20, I gave it reluctantly, yet knowing before the night was over he would be asking for another $20. Who puts $20 in a gas guzzler knowing that's not enough to do anything with, why not just fill it up? As he went to pay for gas, I intentionally dropped my phone on the floor on the driver side, so that I can place the tracking device in. I felt like private detective J☺, for I knew everywhere the truck was at any given time. I could care less where he was or who he was with my only concern was getting the truck back to trade it in.

I had stopped paying the insurance a long time ago, the tags were dead, the repo man was looking for this truck just as much as I was. I called my line-sister and asked her to pray for me.

I'm not sure what she prayed, but a week later, the truck was stopped on a one-way road for an extended period of time. That morning, I drove to where the vehicle was to check on it, but actually was checking to see if this was a good time to steal my own truck. Well, at least I got my truck back but where was he?

Lies Unfold...

It's been two weeks. I received a collect call asking me to get him out of jail. "You want me to do what? Why are you in jail? What are they saying? Where's the truck? I need you, Jackie, get me out, please. Now this ninja needs me, but he f*^#$@ over me. Thank God, my mental plan was working to help break me away from people that were breaking me. This is when I knew God was answering my prayers.

His mom called asking what's going on and would I be able to come up with the money for his bail. My answer was simple, I don't know and no. There was a warrant for his arrest for back child support and suspended license. Child support? But he claimed to have no children!

I really had no idea who I was dealing with. He had three kids and he was living with a woman, who I couldn't verify if that was his wife or not. His family didn't deal with him. He was a liar, thief, a bon-a-fide con artist. His family began to reveal news to me that had me in complete awe.

He wasn't an ex-football player or even Greek. I became enraged with hate, anger, betrayal, and bitterness all over again. How could someone, take advantage of me, like this? How could I let him? I can't believe I didn't see any of this coming. I received another call from the liar, "I'm sorry, please come see me, I am going to fix everything." Ready to complete this chapter in my life, I went to see him. Visiting someone in jail was humiliating and embarrassing to me and I kept asking myself, "how did I get here?" He continued to ask about his bail and I told him I didn't have $5,000 to pay, I was already in deep debt behind his false promises. I already knew more than he thought I did. When I asked why he was arrested, he had the nerve to say it was mistaken identity. Understand at this point, I was asking just enough questions to entertain myself and laugh on the inside on whatever came out of his mouth. He promised to fix it all, pay me back double, and everything will be back better than it was.

I gave him a final smirk and said, "okay, I will do what I can". He thanked me, said "I love you, you are so good to me." I got up and said "I know" and walked away, even angrier and crushed before getting there. That was my last time seeing him.

Discipline Your Disappointments...Do Whatever It Takes.

Meanwhile, I thank GOD for getting me out when He did. I was determined to get back on track and not be defeated by this setback; therefore, I did what was necessary, paid everything off to ensure I got back to living my best life.

Yes, I was hurt and disappointed, but I knew I couldn't wallow in my pain and not do anything, I sought therapy. I accepted it wasn't my fault and it's okay to be me. I will continue to do for others, not because I am a people pleaser but because I don't know any other way to be because I receive great joy from having a "Servant's Heart". I give because I choose to. Yet, I will be more cautious about giving so much of myself: spiritually, mentally, emotionally, physically, and financially without knowing more about you. Someone can be lost in their own truth but remembering who you are connected to will pull you back every time.

Biggest Lesson: when you say yes to others, make sure you are not saying no to yourself.

"Life becomes easier when you learn to accept an apology you never got." ~ Robert Brault.

Jackie M. Brooks is a transformational author, poet, Delta Soror, forex financial coach, counselor, professional/personal development trainer, and Human Resources Specialist delivering mind shifting talks that disrupts the normal pattern of thinking. Born in Washington, DC, this Counseling Psychology graduate of Bennett College and Bowie State University is passionate about seeing others grow and get the most out of life experiences.

She is not a party of one when it comes to serving others. Jackie surrounds herself with a dynamic group of leaders, mentors and associations for positive influences amongst her community.

Her close connections with Delta Sigma Theta Sorority, Inc., Trade Nation, NAACP, the National Urban League, First Baptist Church of Glenarden, and Alumnae associations keep her true to being a servant and friend transforming many lives.

When Jackie is not working, she enjoys spending time with her family and friends, reading, bowling, and traveling the world. Her infectious smile keeps her remembering to never be a prisoner of your past. It was just a lesson, not a life sentence.

Stay connected with me on Facebook @ jackie.brooks.9440

CHAPTER 10

BREAKTHROUGH

by Keyona Squire

"Appreciate where you are in life, even if it's not where you want to be every season serves a purpose." - Keyona Squire

Growing up I was that high school girl living that "fast life," wanting to act up in school, wanting to chase behind boys, easily influenced to do what the "average teenager" was known for doing. I grew up smoking, drinking, and partying.

I wanted to live my life the way I wanted to. One thing for sure was that I loved working; there was something about having my own money. Getting my nails done, shopping, not really having any bills because I was a teenager, but being able to take care of myself. What I enjoyed doing most was pampering myself and hanging with my family and friends. After high school, I wanted to attend South Carolina State University to obtain a Nursing/Health Science degree. While in college, I still carried on doing the things I had done in high school, while maintaining grades and a job. One job grew to two jobs. The more I started working, the less interest I had in entertaining other things.

Within my Sophomore year of college, I met someone who I felt was "the one." I put this guy before anything and everything. I would take days off of work, leave campus, and spend weekends with him. But it always felt like the relationship was too good to be true. I continued to give this guy my all; I was beginning to love him more than myself. Over time, the relationship took a 180-degree turn. He became abusive. I never could imagine being in the position I was in. When we hear and see online and on TV people getting abuse, we automatically say, "I could never be in a relationship like that," or "I could never let someone hit on me," but TRUST ME from experience, its hard getting out of something that you're so deep into.

Things got so bad and scary, I didn't know how I could escape someone so much stronger than me, someone so abusive, someone so aggressive and controlling. I was beginning to lose myself, I was beginning to question life, I was so confused as to what got me to where I was. I was in a situation that I could no longer control. I wanted a change so bad. I had no other choice but to look to GOD and I began praying harder than I had ever prayed before. I began asking for protection, for guidance, and for him to place me on the route he wanted me to take.

My relationship with God was my number one priority at this time in my life. I needed HELP. I was beginning a new school year, moving into my first spot with my roommate, my parents bought me a car, I was still working two jobs, and I needed to get out of my current situation. I continued to do what I was supposed to. I slowly felt myself distancing from this current relationship, no matter how hard he tried communicating with me. I had to always remember what I was praying for, and that the only way things would work is if I obeyed what I felt God was telling me.

Shortly after getting out of this relationship, I got in a head-on car accident that was life- changing. My car was a total loss. I saw my life flash before my eyes. I was so scared and traumatized about what just took place.

By the grace of God, I got out of my car with only a SCRATCH on my arm, and from that point on I knew it was no one but God: he saved me. I had zero family in this city, I was crying in the arms of an angel who made sure I got to the hospital and called my parents. She was a minister. I had no choice but to believe that she was heaven-sent. After all I was going through and the road I was headed down, I truly believe everything happened for a reason. God was telling me to “slow down.” That’s a message I’ve been hearing all my life from my dad especially. As I said before, I had always ignored what advice others gave me, but from that point on I wanted to change my habits. I was blessed to even still be here!

As time went on I began to do ROTC. I had plans to become an officer. I continued to work, partied less, and felt like a change was slowly approaching. I knew I was at my breakthrough. God had given me a second chance, so I was determined to make the best of it the right way. The more I was beginning to do what I was supposed to, the more time I dedicated to GOD, the more I saw him working, I begin to feel like I wasn’t supposed to be where I was. I wanted to leave the current school I was attending and study elsewhere, where I could have more opportunities while in school at the same time.

As soon as 2014 approached and I was well over my previous relationship, I met a young man who to me was the most handsome person ever. Ever since the day I saw him and spoke to him for the first time, I fell in LOVE. From the conversations we had with each other to the ambitious things he had going on, I admired that he was so hard working. Compared to the guys I was used to; he was the complete opposite. I had to get to know him more! The sad part was, he would be graduating within the next few months. I began thinking it was another too-good-to-be- true type relationship, but my relationship with God was so strong I had to trust him on this one. He graduated school and had plans to relocate. As much as I wanted to leave the current school we were at, I felt like this would be a great opportunity for me to leave with him. We moved and got a place together, we both worked, and I was still in school and doing ROTC, because deep down inside I really wanted to go into the military. At the same time, we had to get his dreams up and running. I have never witnessed someone close to me write down their dreams and make them come true as fast as he did. He became my best friend and motivator, and later my fiancé; someone who pushed me and wanted to see me become better. The power of having two people motivate each other can be life changing itself. He helped me grow the entrepreneur mindset.

Even though I had plans, I knew God had bigger plans—I just had to trust the process. It helped nourish me to become the person I am today.

Then, after he had gotten the hang of running his businesses and I was working, I got pregnant. I had to stop ROTC. I was no longer interested in working because my body was tired. I stopped attending school. I felt like my life was going downhill again, but I still kept my faith and leaned on the Lord. I knew he had me and that greater was still coming.

Like they say, this was just a setback for a major comeback, and things get worse before they get better. Having no income with a child on the way was so depressing. But what I did have was a strong support system in my parents, family, friends, and a man who was still working hard on his dreams. I continued to support him and was able to use the time alone to work on my own dreams. The entrepreneur mindset began to kick in when I least expected it to. I was out here customizing, making everything from shirts, wine glasses, decals, and wall décor. I was enjoying making others happy, and seeing the outcomes of their orders was a beautiful thing. I had extra income flowing in and it was even more meaningful because I had started it on my own.

With me knowing I could do that, I started thinking of what I could do next.

Interior Designing always seemed to amaze me, so after my daughter was born, I pursued a career in real estate. In my first year as a Realtor, I had over 3million in sales, which was a major accomplishment. During my second year, I wanted to network and get more involved with the community; I wanted to grow and continue to help others. I dedicated so much time and hard work into doing something I loved, and the outcomes were always amazing. By working for myself, I am able to maintain being a full-time mom, spend time with my family, enjoy my friends, and continue to support the man I started with, who today owns multiple businesses. God works in mysterious ways!

After everything I've been through, I am a living testimony that we all have some kind of breakthrough. No matter what your situation is, it is only temporary. You have to want more for yourself. NEVER settle in life, because you can miss out on your purpose and whatever blessings God has in store for you. Working for yourself and others can become difficult, and it's easy to get discouraged. Some may not support you, you just have to know not to let what's around you affect what's in you. You can surround yourself with like-minded people and your life can change tremendously. Reach out to get any help or advice you feel is needed.

Even when you feel like giving up, remember your "WHY". Why are you doing this and for whom? We all have a story, and we all have room for growth, you just have to want it. There's so much money and opportunities in this world, it's a must that we get out of our comfort zones. Enjoy different life experiences, want MORE for yourself, and help others around you get out of their difficult situations. Where you are can be inspiring to your peers. So many people are watching you, they see where you've been and where you're going. Think about how many people around you that you can change, but it just starts with you. Speak miracles into your life, because ANYTHING IS POSSBLE. Whether it's a new job opportunity, new relationship, starting a new business, finding financial freedom: remember that you can do it as long as you put your mind, faith, and hard work into it. You will be where you need to be mentally, physically and spiritually. Let's continue to build each other and use the resources around us to become better, because if one person can do it so can you. Stay strong and remember that with GOD all things are possible. Whenever you are tempted to give up, your breakthrough is probably just around the corner.

Keyona Squire is an extraordinary powerhouse and native of Columbia, South Carolina. Her unwavering faith, that God has a plan for her life, is the driving force in her life. Keyona has reached a place of true happiness in her personal and entrepreneurial life.

Keyona is a top Realtor in South Carolina and Georgia. Her community work and purposeful transformations, will continue to top the charts. Keyona is a passionate entrepreneur excited about supporting others and inspiring others to win in life. When she is not working, she enjoys home decorating, spending time with her fiancé, her daughter family and friends. She also enjoys traveling, and spending time outdoors.

Stay connected with me on Facebook @ keyona.squire

CHAPTER 11

YOUR BEST VERSION

by Micola K. Glasgow

There comes a time in your life when you have to DECIDE who you will become. During this time, you have to know who you will mimic, who inspires you, what inspires you, and, most importantly, what is your WHY for making things happen. We don't realize when growing up that you're not only becoming an individual with experiences, you're becoming the person that everyone else will have to deal with as well.

When you become an adult, a lot of responsibilities are given to you because of your age, however you may not be mature enough to deal with certain responsibilities.

Growing up in DC with my grandmother, I was always taught these cliché sayings:

“Speak when spoken to”, “Don’t come in the house without going to wash your hands first”, “If you can “huh” you can hear”, “Let go and Let God.”

We all know these clichés. It’s time for us to unlearn to learn to relearn and not just let life pass us by, as these clichés have done over the years. Now with that being said...it’s time that we become the very best versions of ourselves to live out the best of our lives for the rest of our lives. There are always people who will not agree with your decisions. There will also be people who will support you. We want them all around to watch our journeys.

Now, I can remember many days wondering what would I be when I grew up. I didn’t really know, but I didn’t want the career of the people around me. I can remember taking my first typing test for a job. My mother worked at this publishing company and I wanted to apply there, but you needed to type at least 40 wpm.

I thought I had been practicing, but when it came time for me to take the test, I bombed horribly. I couldn't believe it because I just knew that I would pass with flying colors. That was a reality check for me because at that very moment, I realized that I didn't really want it bad enough. After trying several different careers, I chose to go to college to first get my Associates Degree in Computer Hardware and then go back to get my Bachelor's Degree in Computer Networking.

While I was in college my sister introduced me to the industry of Network Marketing. This opened my eyes to another mindset, another level of lifestyle, and more importantly, having something different to look at for my future. What I learned over time is that you have to visualize your goals before you actually see it physically. Over the years, I have had several mentors; however, I never hired a coach until I DECIDED who I wanted to be. There were some very difficult, yet extremely important steps, I needed to take to help soar my life into a new direction. When you are becoming your best version, you need to have a clear plan in mind.

5 Steps to Becoming Your Best Version:

- Setting Goals
- De-clutter

- Get A Mentor and/or Coach
- Study Personal Development
- Get an Accountability Partner

Setting Goals

You have to be very specific about what it is that you want. My mentor informed me that you have to write down your goals and be very specific. One of the things I wrote down in my 20s was that I wanted to make 6 figures before the age of 30. I had to write it on index cards and hang them all over the house. I remember vividly when I wrote it down, but I didn't realize until I was 40 that I had actually accomplished that goal early in my career. I had been making 6 figures since I was 26. I had not realized that I had manifested this goal in my life long before it actually happened. I remember another one of my goals was to purchase a brand-new car, and that happened as well. I purchased a customized 2010 BMW 535i in 2009. I was so proud of myself because I had stayed focused; however, with all the goals I had accomplished I wasn't being grateful as well. Just know that when you accomplish your goals, you did not do it alone.

Now my goal-setting is quite different. Once you know what your goals are...WRITE THEM DOWN!! You can work hard with your activity, but if you're not looking at your goals daily they can be forgotten. Not only do I challenge you to write them down but I challenge you to write them daily. Use SMART goals to get it done. SMART is an acronym that stands for: Specific Measurable Attainable Relevant Time. This means be specific on what goals you want to accomplish and make sure they are written with the "What" and "Why" in mind. Measurable meaning that you are able to track the progress of your goals. Attainable means it will stretch you and challenge you, but with a plan it can be done. Relevant means it's going to help you get to where you're wanting to go. Time is the date on your goal will be accomplished.

Once you have your goals written down, print out pictures to visualize them. Put these goals and pictures around you so that they will start to manifest in your life. It's just like when you purchase a car and then next thing you know "your car" is everywhere and everyone is driving it. This is a discipline that you will adopt in the process of becoming your best version.

Declutter

Declutter means to me getting rid of things and people that you do not need. We have things that we need to donate, we have spaces that we need to clear in our homes, we have clothes that no longer fit, and last but not least those negative people that are unsupportive. Sometimes we have to leave people and family behind. I remember seeing this little message and it made so much sense so I want to share it with you....

> *"Clutter is not just physical stuff. It's old ideas, toxic relationships, and bad habits. Clutter is anything that does not support your better self." – Eleanor Brown*

This could be a hard pill to swallow, but when you declutter you are able to have clarity. Your ideas will flow freely through you. Remember when you leave people that you can always circle back for them. It took me almost a month to go through old documents, donate clothes that my children and I could no longer fit, furniture that I was not utilizing and people who were not going towards the same type of lifestyle that I was striving towards.

Find A Mentor and/or Coach

Obtaining a mentor and coach will help you go to the NEXT LEVEL and become your best version. Your mentor should be someone who has the results that you are looking for in your life. You don't realize that we have been following the same paradigms that were instilled in us as children. A mentor will help you to move from where you are to where you want to be. When I found my mentor, it wasn't until I decluttered that I realized I could achieve so much more if I had the correct guidance.

Your mentors will encourage you and your coaches will hold you accountable. There will be people who will push you to the next level and there will be others who will guide you to reach your highest potential. I had a coach and mentor at the same time because I wanted to completely change my paradigm. When I say I changed, I changed my look, how I spoke to myself and others, my activities, my inner circle, and most importantly I changed my mindset. When this happened for me I created my own brand name, Lady Boss Vibes, which is a clothing line for women entrepreneurs who are holding their own in their industries.

Personal Growth and Self Development

Personal growth and self-development start with you changing your mindset. Change starts with you. There are books and audios that you could use to help you grow. Start with reading 10 pages per day until you are reading a book per month which is a minimum of 12 books for the year. The more you work on yourself, the better you will thrive. People are attracted to people. When you start to personally grow, people will notice it in your everyday swag and start to say things like "You've changed".

Accountability

When you want to change, you need someone around you that will hold you accountable for the actions that you take. You have to make the decision that you are committed to you. Once you decide that you are focused on achieving your goals, you start to become your best version. Having an accountability partner will help you to stay on track when you get distracted.

Your Best Version

Let's start with "Change is good." When you are becoming your best version, you cannot worry about other people's opinions because that's none of your business. You have to know that you are enough. You have to believe in yourself more than anyone else. When you decide to embrace your journey, YOU WILL BECOME YOUR BEST VERSION!!!

Believe Bigger and Celebrate Your Success....

"There comes a time in your life when you have to DECIDE who you will become." Those are the words echoed by Washington, DC born, serial entrepreneur, mentor, and visionary, Micola K. Glasgow.

From a very young age, she's been relentless and determined with helping others, as well as herself. She inspires people to become their best version of themselves through personal development, financial education, and lifestyle change. This extraordinary powerhouse is not a party of one when educating people on how to multiply their money. Her team supports and educates people on learning the rules of money.

Applying her career background in computer forensic engineering to network marketing, she has further created strategies that systematically assist with building a brand, internet marketing, and building and scaling a simple business model.

Outside of work, Micola enjoys being a mother to two beautiful children, traveling the world, and constantly striving to build a dynamic legacy for her family. She has taken the time to learn the rules of the wealthy and her mission is to share them with the world.

Stay connected with me on Facebook @ MicolaKGlasgow

CHAPTER 12

TEARING APART A BOX OF LIMITING BELIEFS

by Maryanna Eva Lanham

This story is my story. I never thought it was important for me to share the lessons I've learned until five years ago when I discovered I was living in a box. Part of tearing that box apart is sharing my story with other women.

The first thing that I can remember is being made fun of and bullied as a kid. I remember my best friend defending me to the other kids who called me weird by saying, "She's not weird! She's different." And I was like, "I don't know if *that's* really helpful."

My parents served as foster parents to a total of about 30 kids living in our home, not at the same time, but in and out over the years. The gaining of relationships and the loss of relationships over the years had a pretty big impact on how I saw the world. By the time I was a teenager, I was suffering from terrible heartburn, Irritable Bowel Syndrome, and a hiatal hernia. By the end of high school, I started experimenting with drugs that resulted in a two-year addiction to crystal meth. When I was 21, a very close friend from childhood committed suicide. Shortly after, I was in a car accident that broke both of my arms and, in my mid-twenties, was involved in another accident as a pedestrian. Throughout this time period, I acquired four concussions, suffered four bouts of pancreatitis, and was hospitalized three times due to extreme depression and anxiety causing me to have suicidal ideations. One of the times I was making plans and was hospitalized for two weeks. After I was released, I was put on long-term disability which lasted six months. During the long-term disability, I was diagnosed with bipolar disorder and was on all the medications that go along with that.

But I don't believe any of those things are what make my story. What makes my story is that all of those items for a very long time created a small box around me made of limiting beliefs. Each side of the box had a different definition, so that the top of the box was I WON'T because "I'm damaged," because "I don't know how," because "I'm not good enough." One of the sides of the box was I'M NOT SUPPOSED TO because I had lost a friend and I wanted to lose myself, and because I had bipolar disorder so "I'm not supposed to challenge myself." Another side of the box was I CAN'T because of all my physical and mental health problems and the plethora of medications that went along with them. And the bottom of the box was I SHOULDN'T, because "I've been broken" as a result of the car accidents and the concussions, because "I'm too clumsy" and "I'm too fragile." I believed the only way for me to be safe was to be inside of this box. I saw the box as being comfortable, secure, and safe. Those four sides were how I was defined. I never saw myself outside of those categories. There was no way out of the box; I should be grateful for what life I had been given, no matter how incomplete.

One of the things that had created the box, the bipolar disorder, was a very consuming piece of it.

I wanted to stay on the line in the middle of the road between mania and depression, because I didn't want to die, not because I saw the value in my own life—I didn't—but because I didn't want to hurt my friends or my family. About five years ago when I was at a doctor's visit, the doctor went over a list of the manic side symptoms of someone with bipolar disorder, and I did not have any of those symptoms. Then the doctor said to me, "I'm sorry, but you are not bipolar. You do have Major Depression and anxiety. A large population of the U.S. and the world has that diagnosis." That revelation created a window in the box that I didn't even know could have a window. I started questioning all the labels that were defining me: what other windows was I missing?

I realized that I was living my life in FEAR: False Evidence Appearing Real. Maybe the box in my mind that was there to keep me secure was actually keeping me from being challenged. Maybe it was there to keep me safe, but it inhibited me from living a true life. Maybe it was there to comfort me, but that comfort was an illusion. And slowly the box started coming apart. I knew that I was living in fear and that my circumstances were not who I was. I started thinking about how I was defining myself with those terrible words of I'M NOT SUPPOSED TO and I CAN'T and I WON'T and I SHOULDN'T and started to learn that I could change those things.

I was able to do this with the support I had through therapy, reading, talking, and journaling. Forget creating windows: I realized I had so many different channels to break out of this box completely.

This is the part that I am excited to share with you, the reader.

The biggest thing that I've learned is: You are who you say you are. Now, instead of saying that "I can't," I say, "I can if I want to." Instead of saying, "I'm worthless," I say, "I'm worthy." Instead of, "I should in spite of," I say, "I will if I have the will: I have no limits."

And the question is, what is your internal conversation? Do you know that you are worthy and limitless no matter what your story is? The biggest thing I've learned, as I've said, is changing my internal monologue. This monologue is what created the box. They say 80% of the conversations that we have are with ourselves; so what we say to ourselves is very, very important.

Recently I had a miscarriage, which rocked my world—but it helped me see my truth and helped me learn to define my new reality, and I tried to perceive myself in a positive light. The changing in self-talk does not come easily. You will need to recognize some of the overwhelming negative thoughts that come into your mind.

You will have to become cognizant of those things in order start changing the way you perceive yourself. I can tell you that, to this day, I still have negative self-talk. Sometimes I must go to my backyard and yell out loud and tell myself, "You're not going to listen to this negativity that is popping up in your brain." Sometimes I write the negative self-talk down and then I tear up the piece of paper, or I'll rewrite the sentence in a positive way. Many times, I'll call a friend and let them know what is happening in my mind. I think that many times we don't want to burden anybody or bother them with our issues. But the more we learn to share; the more we learn that the person on the other line has had the same conversations with themselves. While you are working with that person to challenge yourself to change your internal monologue, they may be changing their internal monologue too.

The next thing I've learned is to stop putting myself down. We've talked about not putting yourself down in an internal way, but we also need to work on not putting yourself down in an external way. I used to get a compliment like "I love your outfit," and I would respond, "Oh, it's just from the thrift store," or, "Oh, I just pulled it out of my closet," or, "Oh, it's too linty, or too old," or whatever. And, of course, the response that the person was expecting was, "Thank you. Thank you for your compliment."

I don't believe that anybody will go out of their way to give you a compliment unless they believe it. Nobody does things that take up extra pieces of their time unless they feel it is deserved by the other person. And I've never gone up to a person who looks ridiculous or who I don't like to give them a compliment: it's a waste of time. So, say "Thank you." Just take it, it's OK. You can take it in and internalize it. Sometimes we need the external feedback in order to reinforce the internal conversations. It's pretty interesting: generally, when women are they're told that they've done a good job, they are likely to say, "Oh, my team did all the work," or, "Oh, I'm so grateful for the company I work for," instead of saying, "Thank you. I really did work hard." And just the opposite, men often just say, "Thank you very much." So, maybe we do have a thing or two to learn from men. I want to maintain the emotional portion of myself and still want to give and live and love the way only a woman can. Saying "Thank you" for giving me a compliment has been a big piece to my own healing.

The next thing is learning to take the negative words out of my language. I was used to saying, "Maybe," and "I can't," and "I won't," and "Because of this, I'm not," and now I've learned to be my own coach and my own cheerleader. We can only win if we think we can win. Once again, it goes back to the internal conversation, but in a different light.

We can always be our own biggest critic and we can always be our own biggest cheerleader. I feel that I have to be my biggest encourager and a force to be reckoned with in order to accomplish my goals. The other sources of support, including my tribe, family, and journal are all ancillary helpful things; but, at the end of the day, if I don't love myself and what I'm trying to accomplish, and if my "Why" is not aligned with my "How," then I'm moving in the wrong direction.

The next thing is not comparing yourself to other people. This one was super hard. I felt that everybody had it so much better than me—I mean, who else has pancreatitis four times, four concussions, gets hit by a car, and blah, blah, blah, blah, blah? But that's my journey, and my journey is mine and mine alone. I have learned to love every piece of it, and learned to glean my own truths from it, and learned that I can be so much more powerful because of all that--not just live in spite of it. I feel that we are all unique and we should not compare our experiences, our journeys, or our boxes to anybody else's. I had to learn not to assume that other people have it better, or that they have it figured out, or that they have it all together. The more I share my story with other people, the more I learn that their stories aren't so different, and their internal monologue isn't so different, and the language they've learned to use with themselves is not so different.

And it's really neat that instead of comparing and hoping that I can be like somebody else, I can embrace myself because that makes me so much stronger. You can't be who you think somebody else is. The only place we can find our truth is internally.

In conclusion, my life is what led me here. But now, I lead my life. My past is mine, and I am who I choose to be. I am not a product of those past circumstances. I am the product of my responses to those circumstances, the lessons I've learned, and who I have decided to be on the other side of those things. What I'd like to close with is something to hopefully help —even just one person—to take your box and tear it apart, and take the pieces of the box and reattach them to yourself to become your armor. Each of the circumstances in life that we go through are what build us up into magnificent people. You can do anything you set your mind to. You are strong and beautiful. Appreciate your past, take your lessons with you, and then let the rest of it go. Challenge yourself every day to be a little bit more like the person outside of the box.

It's fantastic; it's a freeing experience. At age thirty-six I discovered that I was living inside of a box. I discovered that I could have lived a much more exciting life with challenges, but now I am living them.

I hope that by sharing these truths and these lessons I've learned, you can challenge yourself to be that much more and to be happy. That's the biggest thing: just be happy.

Maryanna Eva Lanham is a transformational business coach, delivering mind shifting talks and workshops for individuals. Her passion lies in helping others live outside of the status quo "box".

Ms. Lanham is a partner and financial professional within a Fortune 100 financial and insurance company. She is dedicated to understanding each client's circumstances and beliefs while creating custom plans to protect their families and businesses, to help them save for retirement, and to guide their investment strategies.

In her current role as a partner with the firm, she is growing a team of entrepreneurial, outgoing, and empathetic individuals. She has created the Southern Maryland Group of New York Life: recruiting, employing, training, and mentoring growth- and goal-minded individuals who want to make a difference in their communities and for their families. She continues to grow her team and help develop the lives of entrepreneurs.

Maryanna is active in the Southern Maryland networking and volunteer community. She is the Member at Large (former President) of St. Mary's Business Partners, is on the board of the Southern Maryland Community Network, and is a certified Gals Lead facilitator. Maryanna works in the community speaking to groups on topics related to financial awareness and preparedness, from investing and retirement to college planning, and she has a beginner's presentation for kids to learn how to be financially aware early in life. Maryanna earned her Bachelor of Science degree in Health and Human Services from the University of Maryland.

Outside of her career, Maryanna enjoys spending time with her husband, family, and looks forward to helping others achieve their dreams, as she has done hers.

Stay connected with me on Facebook @ maryanna.lanham

CHAPTER 13

MASTER YOUR DISASTER

by Rhamsye A. Brown

"Our lives begin to end the day we become silent about things that matter." Rev. Dr. Martin Luther King Jr.

It is 7:00 Monday morning and you've already made your day mean something. The question is what have you made the day mean for yourself?

Most Mondays, people wish for an additional day, as if there would be a buffer before Monday. Well, there is. It's called Sunday (sarcastic chuckle, lol).

Let's talk about how Mondays can be magical for you going forward. When you design your day, there is less likely destruction and/or distractions that can take you off course. Imagine a train on a track with or without the planned blueprint for the route. The train will likely have a domino effect of occurrences.

The consequences of the occurrences are determined based on whether there is or isn't a plan and then whether the plan was implemented. Well, this is your life. And no, you do not have to have an architect degree in order to design your life. A day is all you need. Imagine that! You are ONLY one day away from the masterpiece of your design provides YOU design it.

We create barriers and obstacles for ourselves the majority of the time either because we lack a plan or working the plan. I am a perfectly imperfect example. I did not have any direction on my life, no plan on the type of business, career or job I wanted and the result was multiple businesses, potential careers opportunities missed, because I did not have a plan.

I'd show up and that was the matter of FACT for me. One day, I made a decision. I wanted more but I did not know how or what I wanted more of but my desire showed up in my behavior. In the process, opportunities began to show up. I'm no "Holy Roller". However, in the best masterpiece plan there is the "Bible". Paraphrasing Habakkuk, it states write a plan (vision) and make it plain. Ask your mentors and read about people you admire and aspire to emulate. Each person has a story and the main key you'll find is the written plan, whether in a journal, or on a restaurant or a southwest airlines napkin. They wrote their plan down and the evidence you see today is the results of the written plan.

Let's be honest, life happens and distractions occur due to the lack of planning. Destruction typically follows. Think of when you did not plan car maintenance or your children's summer camp costs more than you budgeted for. It begins a ripple effect in charging the costs onto credit cards and beginning the cycle of debt. The initial thought is to pay the credit card off in 30 days. However, within 30 days, an additional unexpected cost surfaces and the vicious cycle begins. The mountain of debt is being established and the onset of destruction is all because of a failure to plan.

Although, you may not have an architect degree, you are the expert architect for your life. Your plan precedes performance and action. The accumulation of the daily activities is the results seen from days, months, and even years later. I've heard many people say if you want to know what a person values, look at how they spend their time and money. I agree, and I always say "The mouth can say anything, behaviors don't lie". Stop lying to yourself about losing weight, exercising, eating better, writing your book, getting a new job, etc. Each of these goals requires daily effort. It all begins with a plan.

I plan for the year and then by month and day as needed. Making your plan this way also helps you to measure how your year was and where you are and where you are going. Today is a new day as you read this, decide. Decide to join me in mastering your disaster. Whether your disaster is debt, work, business, relationships, etc. You have a new day and you're only one day away from your masterpiece design of your life.

Your design for your life is up to you and only you. I'm only here to share with you a little about where I used to be, where I am now and more importantly, where I am going. Don't get too focused on whether you are where you want to be. It's a new day, what's the new plan? As, my father would say, "no one can judge you but you."

Daily life designing is essential to the process. It's the measure of what you go through not where you are that builds you.

It's easy to get distracted. Instead of feeling the anxieties and pressures of Mondays imagine them as magical and create a place and space for yourself without all the other associated triggers. You are now living in a whimsical way about your day and guess what; it's amazing, isn't it? No more maniac and miserable Mondays. It all began with you.

Of course life has not always been this way. As I develop plans, coordinate operations, and facilitate trainings on a day to day basis, it occurred to me that the principles used in emergency management are the same principles we use in life. Have you ever had a difficult time explaining to others what you do for a living? Realize that everyone operates differently, as I had to realize. Talking about what I do and/or documenting it is such a challenge for me. However, as I operate with the work I do, those who have had the opportunity to shadow me have been amazed. I say that to encourage you to embrace whatever and wherever your talents are. And see how others can help you to improve the areas you feel challenged in.

Are you being fueled by failure? What's your focus? Start with the smallest thing like debt. Begin with the smallest amount of debt, so that as you pay debts off, you can see progress.

Are you late to work or on projects? Begin early, start outlining and ask for feedback early and often. I am guilty of not asking for help when I need it and often because I am the one giving help to everyone else, I make the assumption that no one will help me. Don't be the distraction or destruction of your disaster. You can actually master every aspect of your life by designing a plan. Mastering does not mean perfect. It only means that you have practiced in the area and have created a standard.

I struggle from time to time. Yes, I do. What's the point of sharing with you if I am not transparent about who I am and what I have experienced? It does not serve either of us to show you all the gold, if I do not share with you the land mines and mountains I had to cross to get there.

Today, I do my best to operate with integrity and with care with people. I conduct business and operate from the heart first, while simultaneously implementing procedures. I am not perfect by far; however people that interact with me develop a sense of my heart and my genuine desire to make a contribution in the lives of others. As I live life today, life is good, it's good! And I know it's meant to be better. What's the problem or what's stopping me, you ask from life being better? Me, I am stopping me just as you are stopping yourself. It's alright to be good and help a few people here and there.

However, when you are called to help multitudes of people, you will get in your own way because your plan will never be greater than the divine plan for your life. Here is what I mean. An opportunity presents itself and instead of you stepping into it, you shrink. The truth is you operate, as most of us do, on a single point failure system. And that system tells us there's only one way or route to get to the goal. That's our truth; nonetheless it's not the TRUTH! The fact of the matter is there are several sources and resources that we will encounter and we have to be open to using them and being used by them. When challenged to do something new or different how do you respond? What thoughts are you having about yourself, your day, and yesterday? Do you notice that these thoughts were actually created in the past impacting your present and changing your future? Designing your day is a daily essential action. Your mind is powerful and you will think yourself out of your divine calling. I've experienced it and witnessed it in watching others sabotage themselves. Fueled by failure is not a negative, it's actually taking those negative thoughts and turning them around to support your plan and purpose. Fueled by failure is taking lessons learned and looking at how things can be improved personally, professionally, spiritually, and emotionally. Your failures are only staircases. Eventually you will get to the top if you don't stop; if you don't give up.

As you take control and embrace the power you have within, you will find that not only are you the resident architect, you are living your best blessed life because you designed it. You were intentional and your actions align with your words. Every day is like a Monday and they are as magical as you create them to be.

Each morning we are given new grace and mercies - each of us gets 24 hours, what are you doing with it?

This is your life, you only have one.

"Your life is a masterpiece, designed daily"

Rhamsye A. Brown

Rhamsye A. Brown is a Phoenix, Arizona native, author, and leader in her industry, currently working and residing in Washington, DC. She earned her Bachelor's degree in Hotel and Restaurant Management and Master's degree in Education at Northern Arizona University. Rhamsye continues to lead and impact the lives of people all around her.

Rhamsye enjoys serving as an Emergency Management Specialist for which she has over thirteen years of experience.

She has been recognized locally and internationally, for her community involvement. Along her journey, she has received countless Performance awards for her emergency management skills. Her accomplishments have led her to being honored and recognized as well as earn certifications with the International Boards and Associations for Certified Healthcare Emergency Professional and Certified Hazard Control Manager. She continues to be instrumental with effecting lives and helping others master their own disasters.

Stay connected with me on Facebook @ rhamsye

CHAPTER 14

SHERO

by Antoinette Scott

I am the first female Purple Heart recipient from Washington, D.C., who served in Iraq. I also have a Proclamation named for me in Washington, D.C., to honor my Purple Heart.

I served in the United States Army for nine years. I was 26-years-old and married with three children when I joined the Army. I was working full-time as a Practical Nurse.

I had already been working at D.C. General Hospital on the Trauma Ward for eight years. I loved what I was doing, but I didn't want to work as a nurse for my entire professional career.

By the time I completed my Basic Combat Training in Fort Jackson S.C., I was separated from my husband and ready for a divorce. I left home for training leaving my children split up between my estranged husband and a family friend. Those eight weeks of training were long and grueling. I hated leaving my girls behind, but I wanted a better life for them and a better life for myself. I needed to earn more money and I needed more options than working as a Practical Nurse. I knew the Army would allow me to be able to afford college as well as add a new career to my resume.

I joined the D.C. Army National Guard. All of our training is in direct alignment with the Army's training; however, most of us serve on a part-time basis. We serve one weekend a month and two weeks of Annual Training. There can be more trainings mandated throughout the year. For the most part, we follow the need for our particular job or our military occupational specialty, which determines how much we are ordered to serve. When we as a unit are called to serve, it is called a mission. I served on many missions in my nine years of service in the Army.

I drove 5-ton trucks, tractor trailers, Hummers, and 2.5-ton vehicles for the Army. I loved every minute of driving those big trucks—it was so totally different from my nursing job.

I had remarried and had another child by the time I was deployed to Iraq. My children were 17, 10, 6, and 6 months old when I deployed. They were just starting to adjust to our new life - I had only been remarried for eleven months when I was sent overseas. They were cared for by my new husband, my mother, and my sister. If I had been killed in action in Iraq, they all would have stayed with my husband.

My military career came to an abrupt halt due to life-threatening injuries I sustained while serving in combat in support of Operation Iraqi Freedom/ Operation Enduring Freedom in 2003. I had been in Iraq for 7 months before I was injured. I was driving a 5-ton vehicle carrying passengers on the back along with my assistant driver. I was the middle vehicle in my convoy of five vehicles. We had two gun trucks in front of us and two gun trucks behind us.

Out of nowhere, my truck began to swerve out of control. I was in a moment of fear and disbelief. A remote detonator had been used to attack our convoy; as a result, my truck was hit from the direct impact of an improvised explosive device, or IED.

We were under attack and I had been hit by the fragments of the explosion. My chin strap was blown off. My goggles (aka protective eye wear) were blown off. My adrenaline was rushing. I fought to keep my truck on the road. I said a quick, selfish prayer: "Lord, please save me and my troops and send me home with every limb I came here with. Amen."

I was able to bring the truck to a complete stop. I had no idea I was injured. I had a hole the size of a golf ball in my left cheek, visible to others, unbeknownst to me at the time. My jaw was broken on impact and I had glass in both eyes from the windshield of the 5-ton truck I was driving, plus fragments of shrapnel in my face, head, neck, and upper torso. I raced to get off the truck with my M16 rifle locked and loaded and off of safety. I dismounted the truck, took a head count of everyone and was ready to get in the fighting position. Everyone could see I was injured; the medics were called immediately. I was semi- delirious. I thought someone else was hit, even though I was clenching my teeth together to keep my jaw aligned enough for me to speak. My mind was racing. I had not fully processed what had just happened. I was walking in a daze.

I was immediately taken to the nearest medic unit. From there I was flown in a helicopter to the Bagdad emergency hospital.

I never lost consciousness. Upon my arrival to the Troop Medical Center in Iraq, the medical staff began to immediately irrigate and clean my facial wounds. I still had no idea of the extent of my injuries. I had a disposable camera and was alert enough to ask the nurses to take lots of pictures of my face and facial wounds. I was very concerned that my face was horribly scared and ruined for life. When I arrived in Germany, I was admitted to the hospital and prepped for surgery for my jaw to be wired. My jaw was wired shut for 6 weeks. After being in Germany for one week, I was flown to Walter Reed Army Medical Center in Washington, DC. Fortunately for me, this was my home town. I still needed facial surgery. I had facial wound exploration and reconstructive surgery to my left cheek. I woke up in recovery with 60 stitches going down the middle of my left cheek from my earlobe to my chin.

I hated going out anywhere. I was very self-conscious about my stitches and my scar. I also had to wear eyeglasses vs contact lenses because my eyes suffered swelling from the glass shards that were embedded permanently in my eyes from the impact of the explosion. My children were very emotional about my injuries until they were able to visit me at Walter Reed. My youngest daughter, who was now 17-months-old, didn't really recognize me, but she watched my other daughters' interactions with me very casually.

Soon my baby girl and I bonded by sharing milkshakes. These were some of our most precious yet emotional moments. The truth is, she had no idea who I was, and we had to start to get to know each other all over again. My children felt better knowing they could visit me every day, even though I didn't look like myself. I was discharged from Walter Reed on the eve of Thanksgiving, November 2003.

My facial scar is barely visible today. It took many years for the scar to become very flat and diminished. Some days I forget the scar is there. Other days I stand in the mirror and wonder what other people think when they look at me. I have mixed feelings about my scar. I was always selfish in my prayers when I was in Iraq. I never prayed to just live through the war, I prayed to come home alive and well with all of my limbs and all of my faculties. I declared I was coming home the way I left. I never accepted that I would be ok with returning just being alive. I believe in prayer. I believe God answers prayers. I thank God for my safe return considering a lot of my comrades made the ultimate sacrifice and some have suffered extensive injuries more severe than mine.

I have Post Traumatic Stress Disorder. I have learned to make adjustments on my mental capacity as well as my physical abilities. I have moments when I don't want to do anything for days and weeks at a time.

I also have a traumatic brain injury. This means my brain was shaken up against my skull in the explosion. I have moments when I lose a moment in time. As of now, there is no cure for this.

Looking at my entire life, I know I am the woman I am today because of the values instilled in me by my grandmother, my mother, and my aunt. My grandmother and my mother instilled structure in me. Things like making up my bed every morning when I wake up. To wash my face and brush my teeth immediately upon waking up in the morning. To take a bath every night and not a shower, because girls take baths. To match my socks and keep them folded in pairs. To wash my clothes by the load every week and not one article of clothing here and there. To hang my clothes all in one direction in the closet and in order of color and similarity. To line my shoes in pairs. To come home from school and do my homework immediately and not procrastinate. They taught me manners, to respect everyone, especially my elders. They taught me to be appreciative for all things great and small. They took me to church and to the Kingdom Hall. I have a strong belief in God, faith and prayer. Because of them both, I believe in Karma. I know no matter what I do, how I behave, or how I treat people, the universe will repay me. I treat people the way I want to be treated. I do not tolerate disrespect. I have confidence and high self-esteem.

I am kind and fair, but I do have a mean streak and I am working on that. I just do not like to be taken for granted. I do not like to feel like I am being taken for granted or being used because overall, I am a good person. My grandmother taught me to be patient and loving. She taught me to use my common sense. She showed me love and affection even when she had to discipline me. My mother taught me to be firm and to stick to what I believe in. My aunt taught me to have a sense of humor. She taught me to be outgoing and to literally enjoy nature. To smell the roses and appreciate the sunshine and the rain. To pay attention to my surroundings and not be naive when someone is attempting to harm me. She taught me not to go along with anything that I am uncomfortable with. She taught me to say No when I mean No.

After returning home from Iraq, I went back to school and started from scratch. I completed my Bachelor's Degree in Business and Marketing in four years. It was extremely difficult for me. My memory sucks at times because I have long-term and short-term memory loss. I have found many conventional ways to help me as much as possible without taking prescription medication. I take a lot of notes on everything I want to remember and accomplish. I read a lot of personal development books. I attend a lot of personal development workshops and conferences to keep me encouraged and moving forward on my life-long goals.

I want to be a strong example of greatness to my children and grandchildren. I am not a quitter. I am a disabled Veteran, but I will not be defeated by my disabilities. Being a collaborative author with this book is a major accomplishment for me.

Today I am divorced for the second time. I am surrounded by my four beautiful daughters who are ages 32,25,22, and 16. I have four precious grandchildren ages 13, 3,2 and 6 months old. I have my sister, who is my best friend and business partner. I have one living brother. May my baby brother Al rest in heaven. I have nieces, nephews, extended family, and friends who keep me grounded and protected along with my strong faith in God. I pray I am a role model to all who look up to me and a humble servant all in one. I am my own woman. To know me is to love me. I am nowhere near where I want to be, but I am steadily and progressively working on my long list of goals and dreams on a daily basis. I have bravely enrolled in school to begin my MBA program. I am 48-years-old and going back to school is definitely going to test me and stretch me in many ways. I still love school. I will get my PhD. I will write many books. I will continue to travel the world. I love to give. I love to connect people with one another. I love to meet new friends. I am happy. I am grateful. I am dependable. I am loyal. I am positive and optimistic about things I learn. I am helpful. I am ambitious. I am strong. I am kind.

I love to learn new things. I love to read. I am humbled and honored to be able to introduce a little bit about myself to the world. Writing this piece is the push I needed to "Just do it." I have so many stories in my head and in my heart and it is time for me to unleash them all one by one, story by story. I will take baby steps in my writing, but I will not stop until each and every story has been written. I have some factual stories to tell. I have some fictional stories to tell. I have family and friends who aspire to write a book or join a collaborative as such.

I have an infinite love for women veterans who have served in all branches of the military. We have a sisterhood like no other. As I enter this short chapter in this collaboration, I pray I am an inspiration to all who come in contact with me and my short story. I am nothing without God.

Antoinette Scott is a Washington, DC born native, transformational speaker, author, and advocate for women. She strongly believes that there is a hero in all of us and our life experiences can empower us for excellence.

She graduated from Dunbar high school in Washington, DC and received her BA in Business and Marketing at Strayer University. Antoinette served in the United States Army, which led to her deployment to Iraq in support of Operation Iraqi Freedom/Operation Enduring Freedom. As recognition for her service, injuries and bravery, Antoinette has a Proclamation of the District of Columbia, March 2016 named in her honor.

Antoinette is passionate about health, wellness and financial education, especially for women. She proudly serves her community by teaching Zumba on a voluntary basis to the women who attended the Unity Health Clinic of Kenilworth, Washington, DC. Antoinette is a Board Member for Taylor Made Business Professional Services. Antoinette is a Lifetime member of the Military Order of Purple Heart, member of DC Chapter Disabled American Veterans, and a member of DC Chapter Veteran of Foreign Wars.

Antoinette has been afforded the pleasure to speak to live audiences about her experience as a female wounded Warrior. She has been the speaker for Business and Professional Women, as well as one of the keynote speakers for The Women's Memorial Arlington Cemetery Chapter. She has spoken on radio broadcasts with WHUR 96.3 Washington, DC; and NPR Washington, DC. She has done live interviews with former Anchor Kathleen Matthews WJLA ABC News 7; and The Hill TV.

This profound conqueror adores spending time with her four daughters and four grandchildren. Antoinette wants to represent greatness for her family. She has definitely accomplished this, after reinventing herself; not just once but many times over.

Stay connected with me on Facebook @ AngelDCHawkins

CHAPTER 15

WHEN YOUR WORLD STOPS

by Carrie Jackson

Go, go, go is the regimen of life, the hustle and bustle to work and provide. I started working at the age of 14 and then joined the Army after school. The Army life, boy, is it different. We truly do more before 9 AM than most people do all day. You are trained to have a schedule, and everything and everyone must be "dress right dress." Each day you work until the task is done. Some days are early, some days are late; after a while it all becomes the new regimen.

It is structured and completely filled. You think of family and loved ones, but you are trained to focus on the mission at hand. You are trained in the field, and it seems like the hours of training are purposeless. You don't understand why everything is so critical, why everything must be "dress right dress."

Then one day it all hits the fan and your world changes forever. Is it still structured? Yes. It will cost a life. It is no longer just an exercise, it is real. The years of training must be put into action, and you now must realize the true meaning of "battle buddy." Some of us get orders for the war zone, some of us get orders to support this effort. Some of us can resume the old regimen with new controls. The truth is constant, that life as you know it has forever changed. You don't recognize the change because you've been trained to adapt. You have been trained to go into a different mode, a mode of alertness, focus, and mission-oriented. For those of us who go into the war zone, we realize now how real the threat is. We realize now that anyone can be the threat, suddenly everything is the threat. Anything that is not "dress right dress" is suspect. Then, there are some of us who support the war zone. The effect is indirect: you see the casualties of war, you see the capabilities of the enemy, and the importance of why your support is required.

You too have a mission-oriented focus that is filled with long nights and long days because your comrades on the front line need your support. They're depending on you for the intel, for the communication, for supplies, for mail-call—oh, yes, the lovely mail-call. Hearing from family and loved ones is almost the most important thing, the thing that lets you know that there is life, that everything is not war- related or combat-driven. We do not have time to process tough decisions, heartbreak, heartache; it can change the mindset that is already altered by war and combat. But you still look forward it.

Combat has now become the new way of life. You have yet to realize the changes that have happened mentally. One thing we must remember is that our brains are adaptive and they start to reprogram. The longer one stays in combat mode, the more the brain adapts. And when you finally leave the war zone, you don't realize that your brain has rewired itself while you were away. The only thing you know is every day is Groundhog Day. 16-, 18-, or 22-hour or more days. God only knows the tragedy that has been seen on the front lines by those first responders. I remember how every day I would check the list. Each day it grew by 25+ comrades. What list? Oh, the list of Operation Enduring Freedom and Operation Iraqi Freedom Fallen Serviceman. It was like torture, but I couldn't keep from checking. My friends were there. We were all like family.

That's what the military creates: a new family of sorts. One that at times has been proven to be closer than blood. What am I saying? They become your blood. You sweat the same sweat, cry the same tears, hurt the same hurt. You share memories and laughs that others could never relate to. That is the best way I can explain the military bond.

[BACK AT HOME] The war and combat are now programmed in your head. As the days go by, you start to adapt to the normal routine. And it is just that something is off. And while you notice that you do things differently, there's nothing wrong with it. It's just different. You just try to adapt. Then it becomes frustrating. It's like the war is home and home is fearful. The normal life is strange. You know, you must interact with people, but who can you trust? You just left a place where everyone is your enemy except your battle buddy. Now you must love, care, and have hope. How? For in combat, you don't need that. It could be a distraction. Part of you wants to go back, and part of you wants to be normal.

They send you back, and your life alters again. But this time, it's too much. Now you want to go home. Now home is a safe place. The toll has risen past your ability to adapt. You want to cherish more things in life. The military, all the routine, is now old. It's now past time. The only problem is, the pain and the mental war has now become your new norm.

You throw yourself into work to keep your mind off the pain: suck it up, drive on! That's the military way. No pain, no gain! That's the training. That is the mode your mind is set on, until the night terrors come.

I was once told that you cannot conquer what you do not confront. That is why, with addiction and any other counseling, you must first admit that you have a problem. What happens when you have been trained to suck it up and drive on? You march through pain, distrust, and at times sickness. That is your norm. Being vulnerable is a weakness. Admitting you have a problem is frowned upon in this "dress right dress" world. The world is great until you transition. You don't notice at first, you're excited for this new journey, this new way of life. The days go by and you begin to adjust. Then one day in the quiet it hits you like a ton of bricks. The combat, the trauma, whatever you chose to run from, has finally caught you.

My life first changed when I was sexually assaulted. I blamed myself because of alcohol use. I remember thinking, if you hadn't been drunk, it wouldn't't have happened. That experience changed my view of all my male comrades; it became...it became...a part of me. Give it up before it was taken, was the thought process. Boy, was that mindset painful and to my detriment! I thought things got better, but in reality, I suppressed the memories. I blamed myself because I drank.

Simple logic, right. If you were not drinking alcohol, then it would have never happened. I threw myself into the safety net of church, hoping that it would help disguise the pain, anger, and self-hatred that was starting to grow into a tree. There was one problem, my mindset had changed dramatically. I no longer viewed men as the "Prince Charming" here to save the day. My view was they were only good for one thing and only wanted one thing, sex. That is something that I can control, after all the hurt and pain. If I just give it up before they take it, I am the winner. That mindset was sooooo dangerous. I became very emasculating, and when I arrived back stateside it was the new adopted way of life. My self-coping skills were on a thousand. I had truly adapted and overcome, at least that was my thinking. It was great to be back and near family. I was able to see my daughter, and spend some quality time with her. I was damaged though--short tempered, and in the beginning stages of isolation.

Now everyone can relate to the message of this book, so don't feel left out. It is just some aspects are catered to the military because that's what I know. There are people who experience combat and trauma in different environments, different battlegrounds, but the scars are the same. The healing process is the same. Will you ever be at peace? Maybe one day. The champion conquers each day as it comes. Some days are good, and others are not so good. Just know that the battle is won at 11:59 PM.

As soon as midnight hits, a new day has begun. One filled with new mercies, with strength, grace, and love.

As I write this, I'm fighting a battle of my own. An internal battle that requires daily victories, sometimes minutes at a time. I never knew how your physical welfare can add to your mental fortitude, being that your mental condition can make physical changes. But as the dust settles and you're left in the quiet of the night, and all dreams are chased, all vacation trips are taken, and you're finally in the still of the night, that's when you realize you can no longer run from your internal wounds. Like a lion in the darkness, the memory waits and pounces, seeking to devour your soul. It starts by taking control of your mind, sometimes making you see things that are not there and hear things that aren't there. Sometimes it even makes you feel things that aren't real. This is all different, you can't control it. You can try, but slowly the symptoms will show and others will start asking, and you become ashamed. Then you start to isolate more, and anger sets in, fear of the unknown sets in, and you don't know how stable you will be from one day to the next. The one thing you find comfort in is sharing a drink with your comrade or friend. There is an unspoken conversation that happens. They understand each toast and each unsobering comfort of each sip. For many of us, this is the one way to go to sleep without fighting.

You know that it is not normal, but it helps you cope for now. Finally, you get to a point where you recognize you may have a problem. They say, “Seek help, we’ll take care of you.” Then if it is not an extreme wait for piss-poor care, it is mistreatment. After years of being drilled to take pride in your space, clean everything, have everything “dress right dress,” you come to a place that is unkempt and you are greeted with attitude. It is the gratitude for your service, one would say. It can also be yet another catalyst for change that is not for your good. What is known to be safe is no longer safe. You are met with ungrateful people, people who look down on you for your condition as if it is some deformity, not understanding the strength and the courage it takes to continue to fight each day. It is a disgrace that drives you insane, as if you were not already there.

As I write these words, I am awaiting clean towels to take a shower. Sometimes you must look past the present to gain hope in the future. You must pull from that place the personal trainer at the gym pushes you to do the last few repetitions from.

It is now time for you to undergo temple maintenance. You must force your mind to keep your body centered. This may take a while because your physical body must learn where center is. You need proper rest and hydration.

This is key, especially for night sweats and substance abuse rehabilitation. Discipline and focus must be the driving force for each day. If you plan to win this battle for peace in this life, you must train your body and mind to endure. Endure through the pain and process. The mind is stronger than the body, if you train it. Most important of all, you are not in this journey of life alone. Everyone has their own set of scars, wounds, and, most importantly, their own set of triumphs. Together we can peacefully enjoy the pursuit of happiness in this gift of life. We can glean from one another's triumphs to strengthen each other. The Bible says, "as Iron sharpens Iron so does one man sharpen another." (Proverbs 27:17)

It's time to get sharp! It's time to get focused and stay disciplined. What is the goal? To find bittersweet through all the pain. That brings a smile to the darkest scar, and laughter to the deepest wound. You have total control over your thoughts and must give yourself permission to tell your world to stop or keep going. Your choice.

CHAPTER 16

Mountain Dew, Hershey Kiss, and Shade Tree Dreams

by Carrie Jackson

Boy, how I blew it! I learned the hard way how to respect the power of love. I didn't know that one simple question, out of pure curiosity, would teach me the most valuable lesson. What question you may ask?

Well, if you must know, I was standing in line and I saw this gentleman behind me looking like he just finished working out purchasing Mountain Dew. So I said "Excuse me sir, why are you purchasing Mountain Dew after a workout?" He responded, "It's my favorite drink." Little did I know that one question would lead to a lifelong friendship that would teach me a lesson in love. As the days went by and our friendship grew, I never looked at it as something real. My past was full of pain and mistrust, how could I see past it? Mr. Dew, on the other hand, listened to every word, encouraged me to be better in spite of my faults. He gave me dating advice, and showed me how a woman should be treated. You would think I would swoon; however, I ran. He was always so thoughtful, and real. Every conversation brought me peace. I didn't have to be anyone or anything special, just me. We would sit for hours and talk under the shade tree. I didn't know how to process and receive everything he gave. I ran, every pass he made, I shook it off. One time he sent a care package while I was away for Valentine's Day. I fussed him out because I didn't believe him; little did I know the package was lost courtesy of the MPS (military postal service). A few months later I received a box with a card, picture, teddy bear, and a huge Hershey kiss. I immediately called and apologized. Now I was starting to believe but I was scared. What if I was wrong? How could he still care for me after all we went through?

He is out of my league, what am I thinking? So I kept running, until one day I couldn't run anymore. My breaths were short. The Carrie that I knew and loved was dying. It was like I couldn't come up for air. I reached out to my dear friend Mr. Dew via email. Through my words he replied "What's wrong with you? You do not sound like yourself." Truth is I wasn't myself, and he was the only one willing to pull the card. He would say, "This Mrs. J person is okay, but let me know when my friend Ms. Carrie returns." Those words, coupled with my 14-year-old daughter telling me I no longer was happy, rocked me to my core. They resuscitated me, and brought me to this place of life support. I have been trying for years to get back to the fun-loving strong, beautiful, happy woman that asked Mr. Dew about his morning Mountain Dew. It has been hard. Once I was revived I had to walk in the truth and accept the consequences of my marathon race. Mr. Dew was spoken for, in a manner of speaking, and grew tired of the chase.

So now I am left with Mountain Dew, a Hershey kiss, and shade tree dreams that remind me there is hope through all the pain.

Carrie Jackson vows to always find the bittersweet in each moment, because, after all, she's had an endless supply of those moments!

Carrie is a proud veteran of the US Army serving under both Operation Enduring Freedom and Operation Iraqi Freedom. She has over nineteen years experience in Information Systems Management with a passion for identifying opportunities for investment and growth. Her entrepreneurial spirit has allowed her to grow personally, professionally, and financially in the network marketing industry.

As a contributing author in *The Extraordinary Makeover; Hidden Expressions Of The Every Day Woman*, Carrie communicates to women that they should realize their super powers, be inspired to dream again, and gain the fortitude to move through life boldly and unafraid.

Carrie is a mother of one daughter and is know by her family and friends as someone who gets things done. She looks forward to each moment that make life great.

Stay connected with me on Facebook @ gracefavorsme

CHAPTER 17

The Blooming Lotus

BY Briele Carter

Let your "muddy" circumstances help you blossom to your full potential, just as a lotus flower is grown...

I recall being twenty-three years old in my mother's bathroom, crying my eyes out. I was not where I wanted to be in life. Yet, I could not put the blame for how I was feeling on anyone else. Where I was in life and the decisions I made to get me to this point were mostly my fault.

There were people and occasions I had the power to walk away from but chose to stay, even when it caused me heartache. It was almost as if I liked torturing myself.

Allowing a toxic relationship with my boyfriend at the time to drag on so long caused damage to our family. We spent seven years in an unstable, unhealthy and conditional relationship. There were so many high and low moments, I felt as if our relationship was like an endless roller coaster: fun to get on at the first sight and ride for a while, eventually causing sickness to the stomach, yearning to get off, but you can't.

We allowed so much disrespect against each other. Yet, we always found a way to get back together, holding anger and resentment over the other person's head. This always led to an altercation, sometimes even getting physical with us hitting one another. I became angry and frustrated, for this was not my idea of my first real relationship. I was someone I could not stand to look in the mirror at. I felt mentally, emotionally, spiritually, and even physically exhausted of the circle we seemed to never stop running in.

It got so bad to the point I questioned God. This was years before my daughter was even created. You would have thought I had enough strength to leave if I wasn't happy, but the moments were not always so dark.

There had been a couple of years of time invested, so I was content.

I was raised a Christian, faithfully going to church every Sunday. Appreciation for being raised in church settled in my mind during these tough times, because the fear of God kept me in line when devilish thoughts questioned my worth. The feeling of having nothing to lose and being so low caused negativity to run wild in my mind like a child at a playground.

We tried to force things to work for the sake of our newborn daughter. This went on for about three more years, eventually leading to a permanent separation. I was heartbroken when we last called it off, but something in me knew this would be the last time. Too much damage had been caused to create a happy home. Being comfortable in a relationship was not more important than being happy.

So, there I was, recently separated from my relationship. I was a single mother who just moved back home with my mother to get myself together. All the mixed emotions of life had me to the point of breaking down in tears.

I always worked hard but rarely had success. Since I was sixteen years-old, I worked nonstop from retail, banking, call centers, to the mortgage industry. Attending community college in intervals constantly switching majors. I could never stick to just one programmed degree, for nothing was my absolute passion to wholeheartedly pursue to completion.

I worked full-time to support my daughter. It paid well, but I didn't know how to spend properly. My daughter's father and I (whom I had been with since the age of 17) didn't have financial knowledge, independence, or security. The time I spent with him, I didn't grow financially. Nor was I raised to know how to invest or spend my money properly. I lived paycheck to paycheck like everyone else. Shopping and spending money unnecessarily, even having moments of money droughts with nearly zero dollars in my bank account. It was time I took responsibility for my own actions.

The pressure of society and personal experiences in life had me asking myself daily, why haven't I graduated college yet? What am I going to do in my life to be a good example for my daughter? And how did I get to this unhappy place in life? These were questions that kept roaming around in my mind. Even while I did my boring office work that I was unhappy with, I found myself sinking into a hole I couldn't get out of: depression.

I realized I had taken God out of the center of my life! I started to go to my local church, joining a group of peers my age, where we talked about God and situations. It was a small and personal group, which made it comfortable for someone like me who felt depressed and full of anxiety. My mother, being the Godly woman that she is, had been trying to get me to join the group for years, but during my "partying phase" I was focused on staying numb to the world. Other than my daughter, of course, who I wholeheartedly loved and would do anything for. Yet, not knowing the damage I was causing to her for not properly caring for myself.

The church had a wonderful interactive children's center that she would go to during our Bible study meetings. It felt amazing to worship again with like-minded people. During this phase in life I stopped listening to negative music and would turn to positive, uplifting music, documentaries, and audio books. I had found my light again through God.

Weekly Bible study became a must in my life to stay on the right path. During this time my daughter's father and my communication became more and more distant. I could tell there was no going back. For he was doing the same activities that I had grown tired of. We would occasionally have conversations that got me out of character and I would have to get myself back into a state of peace.

I started to date, but I never found the friend or partner I was equally yoked with. They had similar habits of drinking, drug use, or partying that I knew was not of interest for myself or to be a part of my daughter's life.

Finally coming to a place of peace in being alone, I vowed to work on myself as a woman and mother. I always made sure my daughter was tended to properly. She may have been three years old, but she and my mother were my best friends. I stayed to myself because I had trust issues, not only from men, but I felt girlfriends could be toxic and untrustworthy too from experience.

My daughter and I would go for long walks, play at the playground, visit family frequently, and just talk. My mother tagged along most of the time as well, for she was who I talked to about adult topics. I always made sure my daughter was well taken care of. Her retired grandparents, on her paternal side, watched her until the age of two, while I worked. They were always loving and supportive. Then I enrolled her in the best local preschool. It was costly but eventually, through child support enforcement, I was helped financially. Her well-being and education have always been important to me. So, the mother category in my life was fine, it was just the woman in me that needed the help.

After listening to months of motivational speeches from leaders such as Dr. Cindy Trimm, Joyce Myers, Joel Olsteen, and even Louis Farrakhan, I knew what I needed for myself and what I deserved. One day at work I took a sticky note at my cubical desk and wrote a list of characteristics I wanted for my future husband. Things such as: Godly; shows unconditional love to my daughter and me; family- oriented; entrepreneur; like-minded; does not drink alcohol, smoke cigarettes, or do drugs was a must; good communicator; and wants children, etc. I stuck that sticky note in a place where I reviewed it frequently, until I found the person that met or exceeded my expectations of what I deserved and needed in my life as a partner and father-figure.

A few weeks later my mother called, shortly after I had a heated argument with my daughter's father. She wanted to introduce me to a business she was in through someone my age. While advising me, she had informed him of the challenges I was overcoming from my previous relationship and felt I could use a friend/peer to talk to. I was in a bad mood and did not want to be bothered with, but I agreed to allow her business partner to call me. A mother knows her child. When she sees a child trying but not getting where they need to be, she will step in to assist in any way that she can.

The guy called, and instead of brushing the conversation off, we talked. He spoke about the business, then talked to me about life in general. Through this conversation we found we had so much in common, talking for hours to the point we did not want to get off the phone but had to because we both had to go to work in the morning. The next day at work we talked for hours, eventually meeting for a lunch date to meet in person. Then we had our official first date, which was my invitation to a local play called "Martin, Malcolm and Me." We enjoyed each other's company; it was like a breath of fresh air when I was around him.

I joined the business to try to learn about financial investments, to educate others, and make an extra income. My new friend helped train me, while showing me the ins and outs of the business. We talked on the phone every day for hours, always eager to see each other for weekly business meetings. I felt butterflies in my stomach when I got around him, as if I was a little girl with a crush. We started to date more, meeting each other's families and friends. Then is when I realized that this man was everything and more on my sticky note from months ago, for whom I had prayed for.

By then I had written out other goals for myself, and with faith I was accomplishing them. I had been accepted as a part-time intern as a community activist for a local group. Through this group I was able to help my community while exposing the school-to-prison pipeline. It was exhausting to work full-time, be a full-time online student, work part-time as an intern, and be a hands-on mother, but I enjoyed the rush of all the productive things I was doing. I even appeared on a TEDx youth talk with the organization, but months after leaving because I did not care for the activities behind closed doors (smoking, drinking, favoritism, etc.) and the attitudes of people in the group. I also felt I could not relate to them, for we had different life stories, and this may have been more of their story to tell.

On to accomplishing more things, I was approved to move into my first apartment. It was a small two-bedroom and two-bath 890 square foot apartment, but it was newly renovated, in a great location, and perfect for my daughter and me! As time moved closer to the move-in date and my relationship grew stronger with my new boyfriend, I finally felt unconditional love and that I had the perfect blended family.

He ended up moving in with us, and a few months later I was pregnant. We learned to love each other more, as we still are learning and growing together. Despite what others around us were thinking out loud for moving so fast, we felt time could not be placed on love. We got married a few months later. I delivered a healthy baby boy with his loving father's support by my side the whole time. I became a stay-at-home mother to my little girl and baby boy. We outgrew our cozy two-bedroom apartment, and made a list of what we wanted for our new home. We stuck it on the wall next to our bed and read it over frequently with prayer. Shortly after, we bought our first single family house, meeting nearly all the qualifications on our list. There was the law of attraction and the power of God, doing its work again.

Everything had happened at the speed of light. Within two years, I was married, had another child, was a homeowner, and was doing the job of my dreams (being a stay-at-home mother, finding ways to pursue my passions—with one of them being writing). All of this was attainable when I let go and let God. I prayed, stayed positive, knew my worth, and divine intervention took place. I used to think the saying "love conquers all" was a myth, but I am living proof of it, as well as the law of attraction and the power of the mind. Now, this is no fairytale story or a happily-ever-after.

I feel genuinely at peace with happiness in my heart, but marriage takes work, love, and support. These are things my husband and I focus on to keep things going in a positive direction. Most of all we know all praises are due to God.

Show gratitude for the past, present, and the future, for it all creates you. I learned to not let my past define my future. Like driving a car, if you are looking in the rear view mirror the whole time you are driving forward you will crash the vehicle, possibly harming yourself and anyone else with you. I had to shift my vision to look forward, though my rear-view mirror (my past) is still there to occasionally glance at. My past is paving the way for my future.

No one is perfect with the road map or GPS to life. There will be moments when you get lost or come across a dead end. Never give up or stand still too long, but turn around and get back on track. I must keep moving forward to arrive at my destination that God has planned specifically for my family and me. Through law of attraction and prayer, I will get there and so will you.

Briele Carter is a visionary. In spite of life struggles, she understood the need for a correction. Through the trials and errors of life, she learned her worth. God's will and the power of the mind continuously contributed to her blossoming. She now knows her future is consciously molded by her mind, following through with her actions.

Briele is a native to Richmond, VA, an author, stay at home mother of two young children (Yuri and Natalia) and wife to her loving and supportive husband, Joshua. Her passion is to write short stories and enlighten people through her words.

"To live the next day better than the last", is her motto for life. She inspires to be the best person she can be for her children, husband, and most of all, for herself.

Stay connected with me on Facebook @ briele.carter

CHAPTER 18

BIG DREAMS

by Dr. Rashida Mendes

Big Dreams Require An Investment

After graduate school, I stayed in a basement apartment for three years in one of the roughest areas of Brooklyn. At 22 yrs old, I was a Marketing Manager at American Express and was so excited to start my new career. My first priority was to pay off my school loans and save for a house.

My vision boards were filled with open houses, home buyer training classes, and pre-approval letters so I could move as soon as I found the right opportunity.

Living in New York is expensive, so I needed to rent a place low enough for me to survive and save. A friend let me rent their basement for $300/month. Great price right!?! Hold on.... It had no heat and one tiny window that didn't open. I made it live-able and decorated it with pride using my Home Depot and HGTV skills. I was willing to be uncomfortable for a short time and save money in order to be comfortable in the future.

Every day coming from work, the train would pass through the neighborhoods that I could see my future house. The six block walk from the train back home was most depressing on weekdays around 6pm. I got off work just in time to see the prostitutes and crack heads starting their jobs on the dimly lit streets.

After searching for months, I finally found a way to get my first home! New York City had a home program where they would take vacant lots and build new homes. I was eligible to enter the lottery to get on the application list and I PRAYED. Surprisingly, I got the call that I was able to select one of the new homes and put down a deposit.

I did the numbers and sure enough, I had enough for the deposit which left me exactly $50 in the bank. $50 represented the faith that I was making a big dream come true.

$50 was all that I had left when my friends from college were in the middle of planning a trip to Jamaica. I knew I wasn't spending any money for a LONG time. No vacations, no dinners out, no parties, and certainly no shopping sprees. I had 1 non-negotiable goal. The one goal that kept me lifted up was that I needed to own my new house.

My entire life savings was tied up in buying my first home. I quickly found out that real estate construction is usually delayed. Under normal circumstances it can be frustrating to have months with no status updates. Then the unthinkable happened... 9/11. One of the most horrific terrorist attacks shook the country and shut New York City down for months. While the nation came together and grieved the losses, my personal world was in a tailspin. All of New York City's offices that managed real estate developments were zoned as closed for months because they were near Ground Zero and the 9/11 clean up. The same utility companies that needed to turn on my house lights and connect the water were dealing with billions of dollars of skyscraper damage and layers of political issues.

My little house and paperwork for plumbing and electrical permits were not a priority.

Still sitting in my basement apartment with no heat, that $50 level of stress from the unknown was crushing. What do you do when there is nothing you can do? You wait. I re-focused my energy to see how I could be of assistance and move these real estate projects forward. My biggest test opened discussions for me to help real estate developers, other home owners, and the real estate community manage projects. I ended up starting an entire career in commercial real estate and finance; all from making connections to fuel my home ownership dream. What started out in a moment of desperation led to me getting my MBA from Columbia Business School and learning about community re-development, real estate finance and touching over $700 million in funding deals to revitalize urban areas.

I finally bought my house and got the real estate bug. I spent ten years working on Community Development projects that provided affordable housing, retail space for small businesses, and schools that raised the bar for education. I had been fortunate enough to meet teachers, firefighters, police officers, doctors, etc. Hard working people who make sure their neighbors uphold a decent quality of life.

Many of the same people who maintain our quality of life are simultaneously struggling to attain the American dream themselves. The very people that spend their time, energy and endless days defending and protecting our families, are sometimes stretching to put food on their own table, make ends meet, or even save for their future.

Working within banks and private investor groups, I got a seat at the table to see how money moves. Owning property could make the difference for generations of legacy and wealth building. I was finally in a position to share that there are valid sources of funding for qualified first time home owners to get assistance from $7,500 to $10,000 for a new home. I love sharing my insider secrets so people can fund their dreams today. Big dreams can't wait forever.

My grandmother wanted to own a home before she died. Years after retiring from working on the railroad, she was able to save up enough to buy a house in Queens, NY. Although my grandmother has since passed, our family still has that house. It was the center of all of our family gatherings. For her, owning something meant security and freedom. The ability to call something your own has always been a priority.

It shouldn't take a lifetime to save up for a home. It would be great if my daughters' teachers came back from summer break talking about how they spent the summer decorating their new home instead of stressing over part time summer jobs to pay the rent. How can the people who teach our children about the American dream struggle to pay rent and not afford their own home? How can the police officers and firefighters who risk their lives to keep our communities safe have a tough time saving for a well-deserved retirement? There are ways to reverse this.... Today.

There is a gap between the money and the masses. Every career move I made expanded my understanding of business, finance, and how to solve complicated problems with millions and even billions of dollars at stake. I love creating connections to bring impossible dreams to reality. There is money available to help people buy homes, expand profitable businesses, and support entrepreneurial projects. Unfortunately, the people who need it most don't always know where to look. There are grant programs set up for first time home buyers from community development funding Institutions (CFDIs) that offer funding assistance in every state.

So many people fixate on their credit score and how much they have saved in the bank. Of course credit and capital are important but the most powerful weapon is collateral.

You can run a business and rent an apartment but in that case, you don't have collateral. Equity in my home allowed me to finance bigger dreams so I could choose between staying at a corporate job or firing my boss to start my own business. When I wanted to leave the corporate career and expand my own business, having equity in my home and real estate collateral made it possible.

Big Dreams Require Big Faith

I left my finance career at a $800 billion investment group to take care of my newborn daughter. I knew that whatever I did next needed to allow me to be present as a mom and involved in my daughter's life. It is important for me to be with her full-time especially while she was still young. I decided to create ways to generate income that fit 3 criteria:

#1 - Flexibility with my time and freedom to make money from anywhere

#2 - Unlimited Income Potential

#3 - The least amount of people standing between me and my money

I spent six months researching, watching webinars, and listening to podcasts and gurus online showing different strategies to replace the six figure income I left behind. I consistently heard of regular people making $100k, $40k, and even $1 million A MONTH online. Yes, per month, not per year!... I was stunned. Average people were making life-changing amounts of money and did not need Ivy League pedigree or years invested into making New York finance connections. The keys to their success were that they sold something that people were already online looking for, and they had a way to automate their sales. This was music to my ears. Everything I was looking for to make money and still be the type of mom I dreamt of. I formulated my new plan of attack and got to work.

I love being an entrepreneur. I love being a mom. Now, being an single mother running a business is a recipe for chaos on any given day. Not having the corporate job was a leap of faith but my dream required a radical change. I found my calling for this stage of my life and created online courses, started selling products on Amazon, coaching, doing speaking events, and consulting other businesses. I figured out a way to balance building a business while potty training and having a toddler banging on my keyboard. There are so many ways your dreams will transform your life.

I am glad I was honest about what works for me and did not pursue anything that would take me away from the three criteria I needed to make money and be a new mom.

Also, here is what people don't see: I am a single mom and solo entrepreneur, but I am not alone. God is with me at all times. I am often asked, How do you do it all? The first answer is that I am Co-Parenting with God. Even before I knew I would have a baby, God was preparing me for this journey.

Big Dreams Require Intimate Connections

As my daily routine exploded with the million things I had on my plate and family responsibilities, my inner circle had become extremely small by choice. Having too many people around me actually feels exhausting. I don't have much wiggle room for my energy or mood to be compromised, so I honor a few wonderful relationships that I cherish outside of my friends and family.

The one consistent circle is my bible study prayer group. This miraculous group of four woman have changed my life. Every Saturday morning at 8am for the past four years.

We pray together, share our weekly testimonies, cover each-other in the word, and keep each-other accountable for God's plan in our lives. We have held each-other up through births, deaths, wealth, poverty, marriage and divorce and everything in between. We all need people we can be brutally honest with and share our emotional highs and lows and not feel judged.

One day, I was running late for a team meeting. I was rushing to drop my daughter off at school. As we were weaving around other school kids, I tripped and fell very hard and was laying faced own on the concrete sidewalk. I looked up and there was a woman who was asking if I was alright. I could hear every part of my body crying out and I just said. "No, I'm Not Ok". I could barely get on my knees to try to stand. I looked down and all I could feel was my heartbeat outside of my chest. Through my shredded pants, I could see blood dripping from the fresh open wounds on my hands and knees.

I looked at my daughter and whispered the scream, "God please help me". This was that visible cry that didn't have a sound. The type of cry that didn't have enough hope to make an utterance. When you are faced down in the street, there is literally no way but up. I needed help in every broken area.

This day, all I could do was inhale one frantic breath at a time and cry. This fallen moment mirrored the mompreneur struggle. Trying to do all things meant I was rushing, overwhelmed, and managing chaos all the time. My life truly needed to slow down for a moment. On the outside, people see the polished results, but my inner circle knows what goes into me pushing my dreams forward.

My Saturday prayer calls are my weekly therapy. Once we start talking, helping each other and sharing the Love of God with one other, two or even four hours passes and we are forcing ourselves to get off the phone. When you fellowship with true believers and begin to worship God, hours can pass by without a sense of time. We have only met in person one time in these four years but they know the most intimate parts of my ups, downs, fears and victories.

Big Dreams for My Grandchildren's Futures

I dream that the journey God has placed me on will bless others to surpass their own dreams with boldness and abundance. There aren't enough hours in the day to thank him for all that he has done and continues to do in my life and the life of the people I care about.

I dream that my grandchildren will know my name and be proud of the foundation they can continue to build their lives on without stress over money, a place to live, or their futures. I want them to have an abundant life so they can be happy using the talents that God gave them to bless others. This is the dream that my grandmother prayed for me. This big dream is sewn into my prayers for the unborn generations.

Big Dreams can last for generations. I pray this abundance for your dreams.

Rashida Mendes is a true serial entrepreneur, active mother, business funding ninja and consultant, speaker, and bestselling author of the "Co-Parenting With God" book series. Mendes also co-authored the bestselling book "The Extraordinary Makeover: Hidden Expressions Of The Every Day Woman". This New York born woman is proof positive that you can disrupt any industry you are passionate about.

As a featured expert in the business finance and real estate industry, Mendes teaches and transforms lives through her beliefs and habits that inspire people to choose happier, purposeful, and wealthier lives.

Mendes is one of the few African-American female professionals to have touched billions of dollars in direct lending. While training entrepreneurs as she completed her MBA at Columbia University, she has met or advised thousands of entrepreneurs around the globe who've gone from zero to multi-million dollar profitable enterprises. Her inspiration comes from the decades of insider access honed through leadership positions ranging from her internship at the White House and being around industry leaders at Bloomberg, JP Morgan, New York Life, Bank of America and several other Fortune 100 titans.

Her vision is to help the every-day heroes who teach our children, protect our families, and improve our neighborhoods achieve the dreams their grandparents prayed for.

Stay connected with me on Facebook @ RashidaMendes

CHAPTER 19

DETOX YOUR MIND

BY G.G. Carter

Breaking up is so very hard to do! No one begins a relationship with intentions to break up. The true reality is, I thought God had sent me my king, soul-mate, best friend—you know, the One. How did we get here? Wow, ten years has flown by. The dream of settling down, getting married, and living the rest of my life with my partner is quickly diminishing. Spending a decade with someone you love and not growing can be frustrating and disheartening.

After asking for a blueprint of our future together, I started questioning my sanity and worth. Whenever we discussed the blueprint, he never took it seriously. Then we just stopped talking about it completely. I was realizing that we were getting older and way too much time had passed to not know where we stand. Yet, the longer we stayed together the more comfortable we became.

The security of having someone is good but not great if there are no goals to accomplish together. It becomes a drag, with the worry of an unstapled, untrustworthy, unfaithful, and unfocused partner weighing you down. After awhile it started to take a toll on my mind and body, while slowly breaking my spirit. I felt that if we were not growing together, then we were falling apart. The thoughts of this toxic relationship constantly played in my mind: rehashing breakups, mistrust and manipulation. But through it all we always managed to find ourselves back together again.

As time went by, it was harder to let go. There were moments when I was at my lowest point in life. I stopped loving myself, but I knew God still loved me and wanted the best for me. When I had no one, I knew I had His presence.

I stood firmly on His promises in Jeremiah 29:11" For I know the plans *and* thoughts that I have for you,' says the Lord, 'plans for peace *and* well-being and not for disaster, to give you a future and a hope." God permitted me to go through the fire of loneliness, sadness, depression, worry, doubt, and fear so I could totally depend on Him. I was very naïve and in deep denial of this unhealthy and unrealistic relationship. Apparently, everyone around me knew; they would frequently ask about marriage, knowing we lived apart. Maybe they thought we were just that traditional, but in truth, the complications were deeply rooted. My partner was still not comfortable with taking that big leap.

In my mind, I had been waiting at the altar for years, with the imagination of building a life with this man. Yet, he seemed fearful to fully commit. Instead he bestowed false hope of making my dreams come true. It was pretty obvious that I'd utterly settled for the comfort and convenience of having someone by my side to avoid loneliness, often doubting and questioning myself with concerns of commitment and the talk of marriage. We created plans, set goals, entertained wedding ideas, and attended premarital classes and counseling. We even had our pastor and prophetic spiritual father pray and bless us. With their guidance, I knew it would get better. Years later, no change occurred and I was fed up! It was time for me to rejuvenate my life and examine toxic relationships.

I needed to change my circumstances and environment first, beyond doubt releasing it all into the universe to get it completely out of my system for good. I needed to make room and to create space in my life for my TRUE KING to find me. It's never easy to let go of the past history, but the pain of holding onto the regret of what your life could have been is far greater than the pain of letting go. Also, I wondered if our love was healthy, nurturing, and inspiring or unhealthy, toxic, and draining. I had to work through the mental blockage of procrastination to bring my energy level up to detoxify my life! I decided to let go of fear and to break free of this toxic and unhealthy relationship that has been going on for a little over a decade. Not having him in my life was just unthinkable. Losing the love of my life and best friend was even worse, because of the time we invested and our family memories that we created.

DETOXING my mind emotionally, my body physically, and going on a soul-fast was what I needed! To manifest a better reality for myself, I had to transcend to a higher frequency level. My soul knew something greater waits for me, so I had to move past the resistance and push through it. I had to stop sabotaging myself and my happiness for others, including my partner. It was not healthy for either one of us. Doing something out of love is different than doing it out of fear or need.

As I continued to grow in all spheres of my life and started doing things for myself (going to the gym more, meditating, praying, reading, writing, spending more time with my family, etc.), my energy vibration increased. I removed all negative toxic energy-drainers out of my life—those people who were not adding to but subtracting from my life—in order to attract healthier, more meaningful relationships with people who could add to my life.

Overcoming the forces of my mind through sacred prayer, meditation, and self-healing transformed my life. Incorporating this into my daily ritual is a must! I don't know where I would be or who I would be without it. Quiet, alone time with the master creator of the universe is what I long for. Often in the mornings I enter my prayer closet or relax in my great room, gazing out of the window at the serenity of nature. Looking up at the sky, waiting for the sunrise, I could feel the Lord's divine presence shining on my face. Being totally secluded, I found myself having an out-of-body experience, feeling infinite love surrounding me. I meditated on God's love, promises, plans, and divine purpose for my life, while forgetting about my pain, failures, and financial struggles.

Pondering and imagining all the infinite possibilities that my ingenious mind could comprehend, I desperately desired to hear from God.

I immediately wrote down what He implanted in my mind. He empowered my thoughts, letting me know that I am more than a conqueror and that I will have unusual, consistent success. It was as if He was taking my own mind away and giving me His mentality; renewing and transforming my mind. I was fully surrendering and releasing negative thoughts, for God was directing me to much greater accomplishments of prosperity in all areas of my life. When you hear from God, you must write it down and act on it. If not, the thought will evaporate and you may miss your blessing.

I was dealing with life challenges and all the obstacles I went through by envisioning and manifesting an exceptional life, far beyond anything I could ever dare dream, hope, or imagine, through my sacred prayer and meditation. This gave me a sense of meaning and purpose to make drastic undeniable changes. There are endless possibilities when you realize that whatever the mind can conceive, it will achieve. The book of Joshua 1:8 says "This Book of the Law shall not depart from your mouth, but you shall read [and meditate on] it day and night, so that you may be careful to do [everything] in accordance with all that is written in it; for then you will make your way prosperous, and then you will be successful." I believed God had already turned me into an exceptional and extraordinarily successful person; all starting with renewal and the cleansing of my mind through His thoughts, plans, and divine purpose for my life.

I became conscious through self-healing, which is linked to loving thyself and God and people, after finding that it was very difficult to face my own mind. I focused on cleaning up and healing my mind first to eradicate a lot of toxicity. Extremely guarding my thoughts and spoken words were key factors. The way you think feel, speak, behave, and act is important but it all starts in your mind. For the reason that your mind sees for you, so you have to take care of it. I learned that it's difficult to face your own mind and take control of random thoughts. I had to train my mind to think positive thoughts and was careful not to speak anything negative, knowing that there's life and death in the power of the words you speak. Your words can also frame and form your way of life. So, it was extremely important to say what I wanted to manifest, which was an exceptional life. Therefore, I no longer conformed to the worldly and superficial values. I progressively matured spiritually on godly values, ethical attitudes, and the magnificent continual promise of God's plan and purpose that will take me to my destiny.

I continue to learn more about the power around sacred prayer and meditation, how it changes the brain waves. As conscious human beings, we are very sacred and have to be kept in alignment; similar to an instrument that needs to be kept in tune in order for everything to work properly.

The combination of all my cries, prayers, and meditation was like a sound vibration activating the particular nervous system in the brain; shifting the nerve impulses that move from your mental, to the spiritual, then the physical. What I see and speak is ***not*** my real self; it's only ten percent of who I really am. The physical world is a small bit of reality. The other ninety percent is the subconscious mind, spiritual and unseen powerhouse of the mind, *the true heart of our body.* Its potent layer underneath encompasses the awareness of all things the conscious mind cannot recognize; your subconscious mind sees visions that are an unlimited sight. The Bible says, "For as he thinketh in his heart, so is he." Most of what is real you cannot see but when you meditate and tune into the sacred prayer sounds, it connects you to infinite intelligent energy. In tune, you are raising your vibration frequencies to start seeing the unseen spiritual things of God. That's when you begin to tap into the heavens to receive the blessings that have already been given to you before you were born. It's your divine birthright and mandate from God.

It's my moment in time to get re-focused and re-energized about my future. For so long, I felt stuck on stupid with the same foolish reoccurring cycles in my life. As long as I continued to reflect back on that bad relationship or the people who hurt me, they have control over me.

I had to release ill feelings and ungodly thoughts or else I would begin to resemble them. I cannot allow my temporary pain to leave a permanent, noticeable scar. I am liberated and have let go of old hurts. Now, I know the reason I survived all the hell I went through was so I can win big and finish strong. Clearly, I am divinely purposed and destined for greatness. My life still has so much significance, this is an assignment from God and I have to complete it. So, I say goodbye to bitterness! And hello to my God-sent lovely husband, empowering relationships, and new, inspiring, lifelong friends.

God allowed the pain I went through; it was critical for the process. I closed the door on my ex relationship, toxic, unhealthy people, and bad habits. My mind is wholly healed and delivered from any strongholds, because my past situation was already divinely predetermined. Taking it all in, that I can't lose my mind over my ex because I am going to need my mind for the one who's coming next! I am a firm believer that it's beyond a doubt a mistake to write off a child of God. He vigorously recharged my life, poured from heaven abundant blessings, increased my circle of influential, powerful people along with miracles of the right opportunities as well as manifesting money my way. All of this became possible the moment I set my mind free for unlimited self-potential within. I could not see it before because of the mental trap.

Amen to living a purposed, driven life on my terms! It feels good and so much more gratifying. Thank you, Lord!

CHAPTER 20

THE WHY FACTOR

BY G.G Carter

The conceptions of the Why phenomena came about in many different ways than usual for me. Based on my general desires, I am passionate about understanding and improving my life, habits, development, and self-mastery. Over the years, I have constantly striven to improve myself, while learning human behavior to help convey the information to others. Through this analysis, I have uncovered some core affirmations that I wrote down and said out loud.

I began to execute my plan of action to work toward achieving my goals and to become the person I needed to be in order to achieve massive success and greatness.

Unmasking the reasons behind these personal, guided life principles while discovering who I really am, I've lived by these principles. I've faced some difficult decisions in my life, some of which may even seem familiar to you. These personal, guided life principles helped channel my way of thinking while I figured out the correct actions to take. I authentically followed these principles rather than discarded them when I became apprehensive.

These principles and affirmations go beyond the limits of ordinary life. They are meant to be read and reflected on over time, as opposed to being a checklist that you mark off. As you read each point, think about the truth behind it, about how it applies to your life, and the actions you should take in light of it. I live by these principles to attain the success I dream of. These are an assortment of important life lessons that I've learned throughout my journey. They pertain to different areas of life, from physically dealing with people, to our emotions, to life's challenges, to achieving success, and to handling failure.

So, I'd like to share a concoction of ideology I asked myself countless times while believing that it is already done.

Knowing that I can create my own reality, why haven't I realized my dreams yet? Why am I going through phases in my life to discover who I am? Why did I give up my personal power to someone else? Why do I stay in that long-term, uncommitted relationship or marriage that frustrates me? Why do I let someone else decide my destiny? Why do I let other people irritate me? Why do I continue to allow people who are not good for me to stay in my life? What kind of person am I becoming because of this relationship, and is it helping me to grow? Why do I consider myself a statistic, a demographic that other people are able to benefit from but I can't benefit from my own product, the brand called Me? Why am I feeling like the victim of certain circumstances? Why do I keep overeating when I know the steps that I have to take in order to be healthy? Why am I convinced that this is as good as it gets? Why did I buy into that lie that success and happiness are just for storybooks, or that there is no happily-ever-after, or that if it's not one thing it's another? Why have I done all this, I ask myself over and over again.

I do believe that my self-fulfilling prophecies let me know I am closer to my breakthrough and miracle now more than ever before. Through revelation, I recognized that God was drawing me to a hidden, secret place. If I continued to do the same things over and over again, I would get the same things in return. I am taking control of my life by taking some time for me, and by eliminating the unnecessary negative distractions, the naysayers, the toxic energy-drainers, and replacing them all with positive affirmations. I will not be afraid of being in the wilderness and the process of loneliness, knowing that loneliness is the mere absence of people and aloneness is the absence of purpose. If I know the “Why Factor” and the “I Am” promises, then I can definitely overcome anything. And I can change the trajectory and quality of my life and my environment by the words that I speak.

At times, I have felt trapped in a cycle of the struggle of Lack, wondering if I’ll ever get off this merry-go-round of stress, worry, depression, and anxiety. Then I understood that I could change my entire life by changing my words, thinking right thoughts, and living right. One of the mistakes I made along the way was, I kept talking about the things that I didn't want, **such as*: I don't want to be poor, I don't want to have debt, I don't want to live in this house, I don't want to live in this state, I don’t want to go to that job, I don’t want to live paycheck to paycheck*, etc.**

But then I realized that talking about what you don't want doesn't bring to you what you do want. This is why many of us have been ensnared with these kinds of storms: we have health storms, financial storms, relational storms, and seasonal storms. Perhaps what is going on is that negative words bring about negative results. And positive words bring about happiness, success, and prosperity. I now challenge myself to have courage, to put aside fear and anxiety. I shake off that powerless feeling, proclaiming victory over it all, for God has planted seeds of greatness in me. His plan for my life is for those seeds to sprout, to grow, and produce in an exceptional life of health, wealth and happiness.

My life is finally coming into focus. I know my life has meaning. I have a sense of direction, and I feel that I am divinely getting to where I need to be in life. When I discovered my purpose, I started to accomplish my goals. I started making wiser choices by knowing what to say "No" to, and having the ability to say "Yes" to the right things made me feel alive and energetic again. While conquering my "Why" fears that were hindering me, I dared to dream again with determination by my side. I started to focus on growth and to think bigger than "I Am" and to use the power of dreams and imagination to move me in the right direction, while taking massive actions to prepare myself to do what I finally love.

Releasing my strongholds empowered me to get back in the driver's seat. I have carefully planned each day and will now be able to deal with unexpected bumps in the road. Sometimes I don't feel like doing what I know I should do, which is empowering myself in order to be able to empower others. I then stop procrastinating and focus on my visions and goals, because when I focus on what I do want, what I don't want automatically leaves my life. I have had to face my fears many times and have had to ask many courageous questions, such as: ***Can I truly go after what I truly desire in life? Can I really go back to school after so many years have passed? Can I change careers if I am unhappy with my current career? Can I have a thriving empire after having little to no success with building others before? Can I truly be happy and go on with my life after a broken marriage or relationship?*** We all have asked some of these questions at some point in our lives. Especially if we've been through a financial storm, emotional storm, relationship storm, or even a health storm. When those winds are blowing it seems as if we're going to capsize in a sea of fear. But hang on for one more minute, because life is made up of seasonal storms for us to weather.

Along the way, I've learned to not listen to the naysayers. If I am going to have a breakthrough, I've got to be able to silence the negative voices. Some of us have too many people speaking the wrong things into our ears.

I call these people "toxic abortionists," just trying to terminate your dreams before they have a moment to manifest. So, you have to be careful who you share your dreams, visions and desires with, especially those that are God-given. In search of the answers and believing all things are possible, I affirmed that Yes, it's possible for me to go back to school, it's possible for me to heal from that relationship, it's possible for me to get married again and be blissfully happy, it's possible to be prosperous in all areas of my life, it's possible to rise above and beyond to another level, it's possible to acquire riches and wealth, and it's possible to have complete control over my life.

My journey started with *self-mastery*. Simply looking at my own reflection in the mirror, prophesying, and declaring who I am brought about an immediate change in my self-worth and values, and I now see that I am designed to do anything I set out to do. I stand erect and affirm boldly that: I am attracting positive, influential, powerful people to me, who have all the necessary resources I need to achieve my purpose. I am infinitely stretching and expanding my mind to believe that it's possible for me to become one of the most influential writers in the world. I affirm boldly that it's possible to be a bestselling novelist; it's possible to be a global philanthropist helping all humanity; it's possible to be a distinguished film producer, television producer, and screenwriter.

For these reasons, I must align and position myself with extraordinary world-changers that I can learn and grow from. People who see the world differently and desire to make change happen. I am redefining myself to become greater while changing my patterns, my thinking, and my behavior. I am getting the toxic energy-drainers out of my life in the midst of forming nurturing relationships that inspire, motivate, and bring the best out of me. I deserve the best that life has to offer.

I am affirming that my life is filled with complete wellness and massive success with eternal peace, happiness, love, and respect, while hoping my children find their divine purpose and passion in life. Standing confidently and taking life on while operating in a spirit of certainty, I am positively projecting that energy where I am prepared for greatness and every book opportunity that comes my way, along with speaking engagements, television, movies, above and beyond anything I could ever imagine... I am constantly improving in all areas and getting better every day as an author, speaker, and collaborator of the gathering, transcending myself even higher. I am eager to soar into my God divine destiny, AMEN. "For I know the plans *and* thoughts that I have for you,' says the Lord, 'plans for peace *and* well-being and not for disaster, to give you a future and a hope." (Jeremiah 29:11)

G.G. Carter is a creative front liner. This emerging author, ordained minister, certified holistic health and wellness consultant, speaker, and mother is making transformational moves. Her mission is to amplify the visions and dreams of people desiring to go to the next level in life. She is passionate about sharing the gospel and empowering believers to discover God's unique and design plan for their lives. She is on a mission to proclaim a message of hope, truth, and wholeness through spiritual awakening, as she provides practical Biblical tools that people can apply to their everyday lives. She has a passion for helping others. While on her quest, she provides a lifestyle solution for getting healthy and fit to improve your life from the inside out.

G.G continues to combine all her teachings with a heartiness of spiritual understanding to reveal life-transforming messages.

G.G. currently resides in Virginia and enjoys spending time with loved ones, exercising, reading, writing, traveling, networking, and connecting with likeminded people. Most of her joy is spent alone with God through sacred prayer and meditation.

Stay connected with me on Facebook @ ggicarter

CONCLUSION

The true makeover of the everyday woman lies within her abilities to live life whole and walk in her best self. It means being unapologetic about the real you. In short, be as genuine as you can be.

We all have secrets that we keep and our crosses to bear. The key to achieving a true makeover is knowing your worth and not letting the world define who you are or need to be. Your true authenticity will appear each and every time you unleash the invisible enemy holding you back. That enemy could be disguised as family, friends, lovers, or even co-workers. But the biggest enemy could be yourself!

You've got the power to control your life and it's time to remember this, so you can keep elevating to new levels in life.

MEET THE AUTHOR

Rock stars come in many varieties, and not all of them have a thing to do with music. Lorie P. Woodruff is one such individual, and if you are not careful, she will most likely have created another entrepreneurial symphony by the time you finish reading this. Her personal drive and ambition are typically on full throttle and she is determined to let nothing stand in her way of success. She has proven this time and again and will continue to do so while simultaneously inspiring others to greatness along the way. Her only question to you is "Are you ready to upgrade your lifestyle by saying 'yes' to yourself"?

In the past several years, this multitalented real estate extraordinaire, author of Unleash Your Irresistibility: Secrets To Making Every Man Want You, international speaker, and host of Lorie TV has garnered some major hits, proving she is far from a one-hit wonder. This entrepreneurial rock star has appeared on TV One with Roland Martin and several radio shows, discussing credit makeover techniques; cover girl and featured in HerLife magazine, a magazine featuring inspirational women entrepreneurs; she has won numerous awards for top sales and performance in real estate sales and network marketing; has presented countless seminars on personal growth, real estate, credit repair and business opportunities, changing the lives of individuals and offering them advice on ways to earn extra streams of income through network marketing; and she established herself as a team leader for Novae, a personal growth and self development company of which she had helped catapult in the Maryland and Washington, DC area. By all accounts, Lorie will continue to top the charts with unparalleled accomplishments, not just to increase her income and personal goals, but also with the direct objective of helping as many other people as she can along the way. Lorie is not just a party of one when it comes to embracing success on all levels. She extends an invitation to succeed to everyone, and will gladly assist on the journey.

A long-standing presence within the real estate industry, Lorie was raised in the Washington DC area. She always had a strong work ethic within herself. She was nourished by the entrepreneurial spirit of her parents and used that sustenance to fuel her ambitions. By keeping true to her silly, playful, and tell it like it is nature, she continues to break the traditional molds of female entrepreneurs.

Stay connected with me on Facebook @ hostoflorietv and LorieWoodruff.com

For inquiries regarding interviews and speaking engagements, please email Lorie@LorieWoodruff.com

CPSIA information can be obtained
at www.ICGtesting.com
Printed in the USA
FFHW010639290119
50278723-55333FF

9 781732 986190